# UNJUSTLY DISHONORED

## The American Military Experience Series

John C. McManus, Series Editor

The books in this series portray and analyze the experience of Americans in military service during war and peacetime from the onset of the twentieth century to the present. The series emphasizes the profound impact wars have had on nearly every aspect of recent American history and considers the significant effects of modern conflict on combatants and noncombatants alike. Titles in the series include accounts of battles, campaigns, and wars; unit histories; biographical and autobiographical narratives; investigations of technology and warfare; studies of the social and economic consequences of war; and in general, the best recent scholarship on Americans in the modern armed forces. The books in the series are written and designed for a diverse audience that encompasses nonspecialists as well as expert readers.

# UNJUSTLY DISHONORED

An African American Division in World War I

Robert H. Ferrell

UNIVERSITY OF MISSOURI PRESS   COLUMBIA AND LONDON

Copyright © 2011 by
The Curators of the University of Missouri
University of Missouri Press, Columbia, Missouri 65201
Printed and bound in the United States of America
All rights reserved
5  4  3  2  1     15  14  13  12  11


Cataloging-in-Publication data available from the Library of Congress.
ISBN 978-0-8262-1916-9


♾™  This paper meets the requirements of the
American National Standard for Permanence of Paper
for Printed Library Materials, Z39.48, 1984.

Designer:  Stephanie Foley
Typesetter: FoleyDesign
Printer and Binder: Thomson-Shore, Inc.
Typefaces:  Palatino and Stencil

# CONTENTS

# PREFACE

FOR MANY YEARS the reputation of the Ninety-second Division, the only African American division in France in World War I, 1917–1918, has been tarnished, to say the least; in fact, the division has had no reputation except for failure. White Americans referred to its poor record. Black Americans spoke of racial prejudice as the source of the division's ills. No one spoke well of its military achievements. Nearly a century has passed, down to the present writing, and little or nothing has changed. To military commentators the division's history was and is an embarrassment.

The purpose of the present book is to turn the division's reputation around. In reality it did quite well militarily and would have done even better if it had possessed better white officers—all the field officers, majors and above, were white, while the company officers of infantry units (captains, lieutenants) were black. The single infantry regiment of the division that went into the Argonne in the last days of September 1918 had a white colonel who barely presided over his big unit, four thousand men; Col. Fred R. Brown wrote well and hence could explain himself clearly and seemingly sensibly, but did little to hold his regiment together and gave vague directions to his three battalion commanders. In the 368th Regiment the battalion commanders were a varied lot. Only one of them, John N. Merrill, had any executive ability, and he was an embarrassment to the American Army that prided itself on good relations, democratic relations, between officers and men, for he had spent years in the army of Persia where democratic tendencies did not exactly flourish, and even served a few months with the British Indian Army. In September 1918 his command technique was to fire pistol shots over the heads of his charges. As for the other two infantry majors of the 368th, Max A. Elser could not make up his mind during the first two nights out in no-man's-land, bringing his battalion's companies back to where they started or keeping them out in the dark, and decided, as one could have guessed, to bring them in (Colonel Brown, of course, had not told him what to do). Maj. Benjamin F. Norris in civil life was a New York City lawyer, a logical man who felt that if he gave a command his men would follow it—because he passed his commands to his officers. One could go on from there. Merrill kept his charges together with a masterful intent and took them into Binarville, a group of shelled basements a few kilometers above the regiment's starting point. The other two battalions went to pieces in the effort.

The collapse of most of the 368th Regiment labeled the Ninety-second Division, this despite the fact that most of the other American white divisions did poorly in the first three attacks in the great battle of the Meuse-Argonne, which began September 26, 1918, and went on until the Armistice of November 11. Only in the last attack, beginning November 1–2, did the Americans as a whole turn their reputation around into an astonishing victory. For the African American division nothing sufficed to assist in retrieving its reputation. The division's engineer regiment performed very well. Its artillery brigade could not have been better; so wrote its surprised and enormously pleased brigadier general, a no-nonsense engineer in civil life with an office on State Street in Boston. And in the only attack mounted by the divisions of Lt. Gen. Robert L. Bullard, with the small force he and Gen. John J. Pershing described as the Second Army, on November 10–11, the only division that did anything, took German territory, was the Ninety-second.

It is a piquant story, heartwarming to see what a big group of black draftees, twenty-five thousand men, a large force, could do when given half a chance and a few real leaders such as Brig. Gen. John Sherburne of the artillery, or Maj. Warner A. Ross who commanded the Second Battalion, 365th Infantry, and in civil life was a lawyer from Lafayette, Indiana. This book is the first full-length archival-based account of the Ninety-second Division, based on the records of the National Archives in College Park, Maryland; the personal records of the U.S. Army in the Army War College in Carlisle Barracks, Pennsylvania; and a group of interviews, 740 pages, of officers and men of the Ninety-second Division conducted in 1919 by a colonel in the Inspector General Department, lost since 1923, unread even at that time, which an able archivist found in the stacks at College Park.

One of the readers of this account in its typescript remarked on the lack of soldier testimony, its concentration on the views and outlooks of officers. On this point I need to offer some explanation. The reader quite rightly asked what the men themselves, rather than the officers, had to say about their officers, black and white, and their own hopes for a better future in the United States because of their service in a great war. Here, let me say, is an entirely justified question. No account of any military unit, large or small, is anywhere near complete without setting out the thoughts of the men. Alas, for the Ninety-second none appears to exist. Researchers on African Americans and the U.S. Army have found very little on the men themselves. For whatever reason or reasons, one fears that as in so many important aspects of history, this portion of the Ninety-second's past has been lost.

The other reader of the typescript manuscript pointed out the World War II sequel to the history of the Ninety-second in World War I, what followed from 1941 to 1945. Himself a National Guard brigadier general, this scholar wrote eloquently of how the U.S. Army went into the second great war of the last century with army leaders determined to have no more failures, they said privately, such as happened in 1917–1918. Relenting, the army's leadership organized the Ninety-second again, with careful leadership and careful training. The reorganized division went into the Italian campaign against the German Army, received clear assignments, and performed well. The division of World War I was a preliminary to a new outlook based on reality rather than imagination. He pointed out what would happen later, the experience of a Gen. Colin Powell commanding in action both African American and white troops, a splendid scene compared to its beginning.

# ACKNOWLEDGMENTS

AT INDIANA UNIVERSITY, I thank the research archivists Jeffrey C. Graf and Louise Malcomb who can handle all library tasks; they are a reliance—all libraries need them, and many do not have them. For maps I resorted to the skilled cartographer at Indiana, John M. Hollingsworth. And for word processing my reliance was Betty Bradbury. In the National Archives in College Park, Maryland, I sought out Timothy K. Nenninger, the head of the Modern Military Branch, who when the other Tim, Tim Frank, the freelance researcher, sought him out at once went up into the stacks to find the file in question. The individual who found it, all of us knowing it was there, was the former World War I archivist Mitchell A. Yockelson, who remembered a small collection of cards in the Department of the Inspector General. He experimented with different words in the file's long title, and an unlikely word opened the file. It was a feat of archival investigation.

At the U.S. Army Military History Institute, a part of the Army War College in Carlisle Barracks, Pennsylvania, near Harrisburg, I am indebted once more to Richard J. Sommers. John Slonaker similarly shared his extraordinary knowledge of institute files.

Edward M. Coffman again has been wonderfully helpful.

At the University of Missouri Press my thanks to the director, Dwight Browne; the editor in chief, Clair Willcox; and the managing editor, Sara Davis. Annette Wenda took the manuscript in hand, notes and all, and missed nothing.

Beverly Jarrett's long experience has made a difference. James J. Cooke provided seven pages of line comment. It is a pleasure to be included in Missouri's new American Military Experience Series edited by John C. McManus.

Carolyn, Lorin, Amanda, and Samantha helped in all ways.

# UNJUSTLY DISHONORED

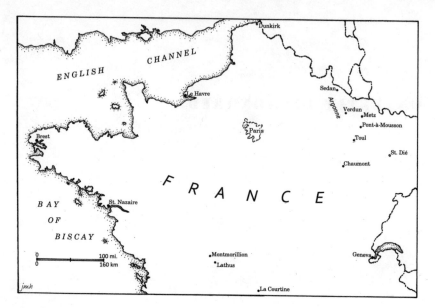

The Western Front.

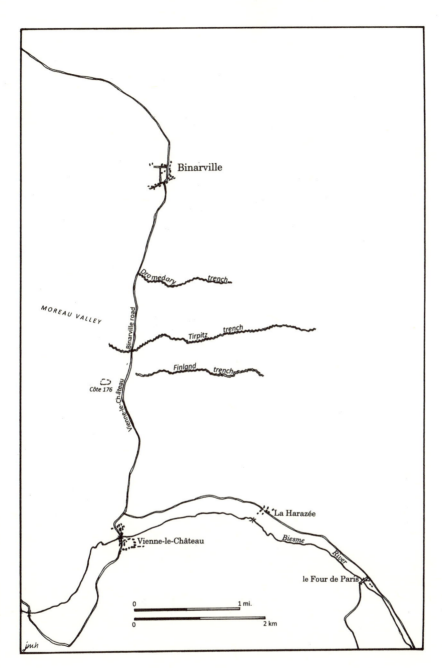

Binarville

MOREAU VALLEY

Dromedary trench

Tirpitz trench

Finland trench

Côte 176

Vienne-le-Château

Binarville road

La Harazée

Vienne-le-Château

Biesme

River

le Four de Paris

0     1 mi.

0     2 km

jmh

Argonne.

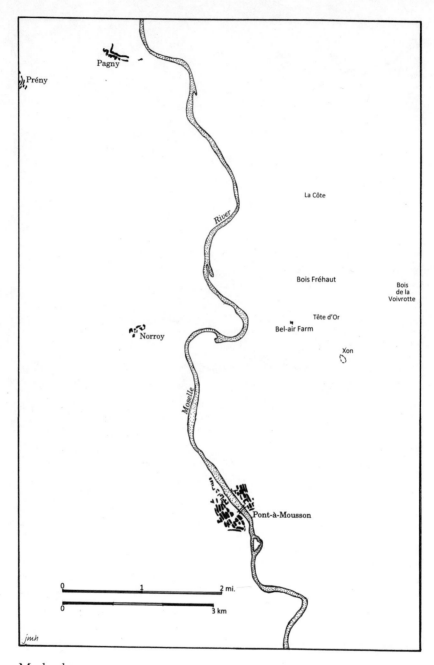

Pagny

Prény

La Côte

River

Bois Fréhaut

Bois
de la
Voivrotte

Tête d'Or

Norroy

Bel-air Farm

Xon

Moselle

Pont-à-Mousson

0            1            2 mi.

0                     3 km

jmh

Marbache.

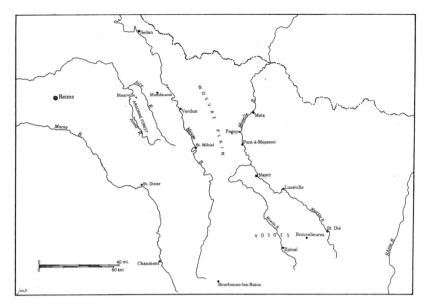

First and Second Armies.

# ONE

# Training

THE TRAINING OF the Ninety-second Division did not differ much from training of other divisions organized by the War Department after the nation entered the world war in April 1917. After its organization in October 1917, the Ninety-second trained in the United States and then, upon arriving in France the next summer, began more training under a schedule set out by the commander of the American Expeditionary Forces (AEF), General Pershing. It barely got started on the new training when it took over a quiet sector in Alsace, was there for three weeks, and left hurriedly for the Argonne Forest.

Two huge tasks faced the administration of President Woodrow Wilson after the declaration of war, only one of which was to organize and train an army. The other was to produce the weapons of war necessary to arm an army and the ships to take the army and its equipment to France. Unfortunately, the nation's enormous industrial plant—the United States had become the world's largest steel producer years before, in 1880—proved unable to equip its troops and build ships quickly enough to take them to France, and for these necessities had to rely upon its allies, principally Great Britain. In the work of raising and training an army the War Department in Washington was more successful, although its achievements left much to be desired, training less than it should have been.

The U.S. Army prior to 1917 had been largely a constabulary force, designed to fight Indians in the West and then, after the Spanish-American War of 1898, to put down the Filipino Rebellion that opened even before the United States annexed the Philippine Islands, and upon ending the rebellion turned into the guerrilla outbreaks of the Moros. For almost twenty years after 1898 the army, which increased from 25,000 men and officers to 130,000 by 1917, took on whatever tasks appeared in the Far East and the protectorates in Central America and the Caribbean, including an excursion into northern Mexico in 1916–1917. After the declaration of war against Germany the army needed a vast enlargement, eventually to nearly 4 million men. The task included construction of cantonments for the new divisions, tent camps in the South, barrack camps in the North. Upon their approximate completion in the autumn of 1917, the camps, especially the barracks in the North, required much work, which extended into the winter.

# 1

The Ninety-second's drafts of new men found themselves in a series of northern barrack camps. For the Ninety-second the War Department naturally decided upon cantonments in the North, and unlike the other cantonment divisions scattered the division across a range of camps from Kansas to Long Island. The reason for scattering was the department's decision that African Americans in an individual camp should be in a minority in that camp, not more than one to three. Critics said at the time and later that this precluded training of the troops in large units. The division necessarily could not come together, nor could it assemble the two infantry brigades. The largest unit in a camp would be a regiment. Cantonments comprised thousands of acres, plenty of room for maneuvers, and the War Department rule on size had its disadvantages, but white racists in the North could not claim they were in danger of some sort or other from masses of black troops in their midst.

Infantry training in the cantonments, one must say, and this included training in the Ninety-second's units, was at best uninspired. The army did not have many trainers, the best of them going abroad in the summer of 1917 in the First Division, for which General Pershing had his choice from officers of the Regular Army. And the army's officers during the period of American neutrality, when they might have learned a good deal about European ways of war, learned little or nothing. A few had gone to Europe as attachés in embassies and legations and gotten out with troops of the Allies and Central Powers. Their dispatches came into the War College in Washington, where they lay in great piles and by testimony of officers present were almost completely unread. A further confusion was that the high command of the German Army on November 11, 1917, an interesting date, decided to embark on a new kind of war that they hoped would take their troops out of the trenches. It would virtually abolish the trench war that had characterized the western front almost from the war's beginning in 1914. The new German tactics stressed infiltration by small attack groups with machine guns, which would penetrate front lines and get into back areas. The German general staff would not allow frontal assaults and would depend, for attacks and retreats alike, on machine guns and artillery. All this required new tactics by opposing infantrymen, and the Ninety-second's troops received no such instruction, relying in the cantonments on French and British instructors sent from the lines and possessing the tactical wisdom of 1917, not what was to come on the western front beginning March 21, 1918, when the German Army opened the first of five massive attacks in a spring and summer offensive that almost broke through to Paris—which would have ended the war before the Ninety-second and other cantonment divisions got into action or some of them arrived.

The shipment of American divisions to France was delayed because the United States proved unable to launch enough shipping—the American merchant marine had shrunk to a low level, one million gross tons of oceangoing shipping—and it was only when the British government offered shipping in January 1918, anticipating the German spring offensive, that the divisions could get to France, which they did in the spring and early summer. The Ninety-second was one of them.

Another factor in the training of the African American divisions and other divisions was the cold winter of 1917–1918. That winter recalled the Great Blizzard of 1873. The winter taxed memories and broke records, and for the soldiers, whether in tents or barracks, neither of which was designed for unusual weather, there was little but unmitigated misery.

The initial need of the division was a cadre of officers, for which the army approved a special Officer Training School in Des Moines, Iowa. A debate arose over whether a black OTS should be organized, the cause of which was Maj. Gen. Leonard Wood, who was in command of the military district centered in New York City. In 1915 he organized the first OTS, strictly for whites, in a camp near Plattsburgh, New York. Its success led to schools across the country. Early in 1917 he offered to organize one for African Americans if two hundred candidates were available. The general was a close friend of former president Theodore Roosevelt, hence a Republican and hostile to the Democratic Wilson administration.[1] It does not seem that he made his proposal to embarrass the administration. He did create sentiment about a camp, pro and con, with the National Association for the Advancement of Colored People in the person of one of its white officials, Joel T. Spingarn, urging a black OTS. Some African Americans argued that the segregation of such a camp if held in the South would be wrong, and Spingarn said the South's congressmen and behind them its people wanted such a camp to fail and that blacks should accept a southern camp for the opportunity to create black U.S. Army officers. When the army finally offered an OTS at Des Moines, one African American described it as the most important move of the federal government since the Fifteenth Amendment. Harvard-trained black historian W. E. B. DuBois declared that when Secretary Newton D. Baker announced the camp, it was the most that any member of Wilson's cabinet had done for blacks.[2]

At Des Moines the school organized under the direction of a Regular officer, Col. Charles C. Ballou, who when the division was organized became its commanding general, with promotion to major general. Ballou proved an intelligent officer who believed in the need for African American officers. He saw to it that relations between the students and local citizens were of the best. No serious incident arose, and the city did everything possible to make the men feel at home. The officer candidates undertook a formal drill in the Drake University stadium, and ten thousand people turned out to watch them. A reception at a place named White Sparrows brought hundreds of citizens. The churches, in a surprising event for the time, welcomed the black men to their services.

The first class finished in October, having been kept a month after the usual officer training of three months (whereby graduates of an OTS were known to their men as "ninety-day wonders").

Secretary of War Newton D. Baker in Washington told OTS representatives that the department had delayed because of southern protests against the camp, especially after race riots in East St. Louis and Houston. The official department explanation was that it had to delay the black draft for a month because of lack of places in several northern cantonments—it could not use the officers until solution of that problem.

The graduating class consisted of some six hundred men, with one hundred captains, the rest divided between first and second lieutenants. Of the candidates a fifth were drawn from noncommissioned officers, sergeants and corporals, from the four Regular regiments of black troops the army maintained in peacetime usually in the West, the 9th and 10th Cavalries and the 24th and 25th Infantries, a natural recourse among the men at Des Moines, with others coming from civil life.

In decisions on what candidates should receive what ranks there later was argument that to commission as captains the sergeants and corporals of the Regular Army was a mistake, for many of them had only sixth and seventh grade educations, whereas lieutenants often were college graduates. The answer to that has to be that men of the Regular Army needed recognition for the years, sometimes twenty and more, spent in the military, and that educational standards differed widely, with some grade schools certainly equal to high schools; many college degrees of the time were from very small and almost primitive institutions, not worth much. The officers in charge at Fort Des Moines had to choose some course and did so, and disagreements were inevitable.[3]

The draft of African American men turned out remarkably well, in that there was little shirking or refusal to cooperate. Everything was as orderly as for the draft of whites. In the first draft 6,451,856 men registered, blacks and whites, of which 342,247 blacks and 1,416,750 whites were chosen for service. The percentage of African Americans chosen was higher than for whites, though the difference was not marked: 31.74 for blacks, 26.84 for whites. Half of the blacks qualified served abroad.

As for what they did upon arrival, men in infantry units served in them; the same held for whites. Far more blacks than whites went over assigned to stevedore or other labor behind the lines, units with white officers, not black. It could be argued that the large numbers of African Americans who—in labor units it often was three-fourths—were illiterate militated in that direction, although it was difficult to see that infantry training had any large reliance on the written word. The army had manuals for everything about combat and support operations. Many of them were copied from French and British manuals. These field manuals found their way up from soldier to divisional level. How closely they were read by the men was something else.

Divisional headquarters were at Funston in Kansas, meaning that the newly promoted General Ballou had to direct, if he could, men in all units out to Long Island from the far western cantonment.[4] Just what he could do in that regard was at the least problematic. Ballou reported to the inspector on the period of May 18–27, 1918, on what the units were doing in "the school of the soldier." Apparently he was speaking only of the troops at Funston, not his entire division scattered at the cantonments. The units had undergone disciplinary training regardless of the special purposes for which they were organized. There was also instruction in march discipline and in extended order. In addition to this training, each unit received "the technical instruction its character demanded." Disciplinary training meant saluting, perhaps not an essential for troops at the front. March discipline presumably taught troops the quickest way to get from one place to another but was useless on a battlefield where any troop concentration invited a rain of shrapnel and, if close enough, machine-gun bullets. Extended order drill had value, teaching troops to spread out, but nothing could teach troops to stay apart when under fire, for the urgent impulse for all raw troops was to come together. As for "technical instruction," the general did not specify. The dates for the above instruction, elementary as it was, were uncomfortably close to the time in June when the division went overseas.

A few machine-gun companies trained at Funston. Such companies were smaller than infantry companies (the latter comprised 250 men). According to a division table of organization, each division had three machine-gun battalions, each with three companies. Training of men at Funston in machine guns must not have been better than that of all the divisions as long as they were in the United States, for the army had almost no guns with which to train them. The Browning guns, heavies and lights, excellent weapons, used in World War II and Korea, did not go into production until after the war began and the American inventor showed his weapons to the War Department. In France for most of the war—Brownings were released to some of the divisions during the last weeks—the troops used French heavy Hotchkisses and the light guns known as Chauchats, arguably the worst light guns used by any of the major national armies during the war.

At Camp Dodge in Iowa there was training of the 366th Infantry, a sizable body of troops, in 1917–1918 four thousand men. Its training at Dodge is difficult to discern. When a group of Regular officers, members of the general staff, did a study of the Ninety-second in 1923, using all the records they could easily go through, they were struck by the dearth of records, as well as the vague statements used by inspectors to describe what they were about— officers from the Inspector General Department visited and drew up appraisals but showed caution or disinclination to get into details. Inspectors included men of rank, two brigadier generals, free of pressure from the officers in charge they met. The single report on training of the 366th spoke of lack of winter apparel. The 366th reported zero-degree weather or below on twenty-nine days after December 1, impossible to train outside of barracks.

The other cantonments were all east of Funston and Dodge. The inspector at Camp Grant, Illinois, reported that training of the 365th Infantry and a machine-gun battalion began November 5 and followed the schedule prescribed for the Eighty-sixth Division, also at Grant. The command was in its sixth week of training, and progress had been satisfactory. He added that the regiment and battalion had full complements of officers, averaging fifty men per company, and with daily duties required for all units, guard duty and so on, turnout for training exercises in each company averaged fifteen or twenty.

At Camp Sherman in Ohio was the Ninety-second's engineer regiment, some fourteen hundred men. Training was uncertain, for at that time the regiment had two engineer-trained officers. The remainder were trained in Des Moines.

A battalion of the Ninety-second's 317th Machine Gun Regiment was in training, six hundred men, for what little was possible without the guns. The battalion in late April 1918 was in quarantine for scarlet fever. The camp trained signal corps men, as well as sanitary, meaning medical, units. Here the present writer can offer personal detail, for his father trained at Sherman in a white medical unit, not that of the Ninety-second. The winter was cold, and my grandfather, an Ohio farmer, sent a horse blanket. According to the author's father, Sherman was inhabited by a legion of hoot owls, which each night made sleep impossible.

The 368th Regiment was at Camp Meade, Maryland, and this regiment that obtained a poor reputation in the Argonne may have had good training, but the few reports for January 1918 covered everything in general statements: "performed the usual camp duties, etc."; "training schedules were carried out in so far as weather conditions permitted." In February the weather improved. In March attention went to security, probably guard duty, and minor tactics, perhaps bayonet practice. The regiment pitched shelter tents and bivouacked on the reservation to the south of the cantonment, on the night of March 20, 1918. In April the regiment took part in a parade in Baltimore reviewed by President Wilson.

In rifle practice the 368th and the other infantry regiments stationed at the camps practiced with rifles, their basic weapon, unlike other troops of the division. This meant practice with a few Springfields, the best rifle on the western front, made in a single government arsenal by artisans, and production could not expand to meet the draft levies of the wartime army. Men of the infantry regiments of divisions without Springfields had to make do with Lee-Enfields, British rifles modified to take Springfield ammunition. The Lee-Enfield suffered from a poor siting mechanism.

The three artillery regiments of the Ninety-second, each the size of the division's engineer regiment, were unable to practice with the French artillery with which they would be equipped upon arrival in France. The army sought to reproduce French artillery, heavy pieces and light, but failed. One of the artillery regiments was at Camp Meade. A motorized regiment, it was without its Caterpillar trucks. The other two artillery regiments were at Camp Dix, New Jersey. At Dix also was the 317th Trench Mortar Battery (the several special units of divisions all took the same number). In January 1918 an inspector recommended organization of the Dix mortar unit. The unit comprised one captain and no men. In February officers rose to three. In March there was an addition of two men. April added men. On May 29 the number of men decreased to forty-eight. In the following days there was instruction in the School of the Soldier, the army's description of marching and military courtesy, that is, saluting. Also the men learned the manual of arms. Drill was with dummy weapons: mortars were as unprocurable as machine guns and artillery. The mortar unit left for overseas on June 16, of course sans mortars, able to salute, unable to fire.

Some divisional units assembled at Camp Upton on Long Island. Here the 164th Infantry Brigade had headquarters. The 367th Infantry was at Upton, together with part of a machine-gun battalion. Of the three machine-gun battalions in each division, one was assigned to each infantry brigade and one to division headquarters.

## 2

Training overseas was quite different from that in the home country but in its way just as unsatisfactory. Only the four divisions that General Pershing had in his command over the winter of 1917–1918 reached the high standards of the AEF's commander in chief. One of Pershing's best organizational novelties in his general headquarters (GHQ) at Chaumont, copied at army, corps, division, and regimental levels, was the G-system, in use in the U.S. Army today: G-1 personnel, G-2 intelligence, G-3 operations, G-4 supply, G-5 training. According to the G-5 section, in World War I each division was to train for 90 days, in three phases. The first was training of small units. The second was training under a veteran unit, British or French, preferably in a quiet sector. The third consisted of return to a training area and working out whatever defects appeared.

Of Pershing's divisions, twenty-nine of them in the line at the time of the Armistice, only the initial four, with far more time to train than the others, had all three training phases. Only the First Division had the third phase in full; the other three had a week or two. The First had the most days of training, 192. The Forty-second had the least, 152. The other two divisions, the Second and Twenty-sixth, did not do as well as the First but one could say well enough, if training days meant what they were supposed to. In the case of the Twenty-sixth, supposedly well trained, it did poorly in action, and its politically minded commanding general was sent back to the United States for what the commander in chief diplomatically described as training of troops.

The bulk of the AEF's divisions, coming over in the spring and summer of 1918, trained to lower standards. Four of them had three phases, fifteen had two, six had one.The training of the Ninety-second Division proved to be two phases. According to the AEF's plan, training took place in Lorraine—it was a part of Pershing's "Lorraine strategy."[5] Along the entire western front from Dunkirk to Switzerland the national forces were, first, the tiny Belgian Army, formed after the Germans occupied most of that country during the first days of the war in 1914. There followed the British Expeditionary Force, supplied from across the Channel. Then the French Army ranged mostly in protection of Paris and supplied from there and to the west and south. The plan was for the AEF to concentrate in Lorraine to the east of the French and eventually take over the line all the way to Switzerland. The Ninety-second landed at Brest and Saint-Nazaire, with the first unit coming in on June 16, 1918, the last on July 12. Division headquarters opened June 29 at Bourbonne-les-Bains, in what the AEF described as the 11th Training Area. Training began about July 6, this being the Ninety-second's first phase of "general principles governing train- ing of the American Expeditionary Forces." On August 12 the divi- sion moved to the vicinity of Bruyères in the Vosges.

In the first phase of AEF training the Ninety-second's infantry regiments theoretically did well, although it is difficult to know because of the poor records that survived. A division memoran- dum relates training that was supposed to prevail. No memoran- dum has survived showing what troops actually did. According to the War College study in 1923, there was instruction for com- panies in attack (offensive conduct for small units), instruction of company specialists, range and pistol practice, organization of a company strong point, close-order drill by platoons, battalion defense, preparation and occupation of centers of resistance, day and night relief of battalions therein, sentries' instruction, patrols and raids, disposition to undergo heavy bombardment, disposition to receive hostile attack and counterattack, gas training, security of small groups in isolated strong points, repelling and defeating raids, principles of field fortification, and preliminary brigade terrain exercises.[6]

At the same time the division was in first-phase training the issue of equipment became acute, for troops arrived with little more than uniforms. The head of GHQ's G-5 section, Col. Harold B. Fiske, soon promoted to brigadier general, visited the Ninety-second on June 27, when half of the division was in its training area, and found startling deficiencies: no transportation, no heavy machine guns or automatic rifles, no pistols (for officers and noncommissioned officers), no one-pounder guns (37mm), no mortars, no grenades, and only one hundred rounds of rifle ammunition for each soldier. Three weeks later General Fiske reported an inspection of the three machine-gun battalions, and if other units were similarly equipped they were still, despite his prodding, in bad shape. Fiske found none of the equipment necessary to measure ranges, no grenades to take out enemy guns. The 350th had heavy machine guns but no carts to carry the guns, no animals to pull the carts. The 351st had neither transport nor animals. None of the battalions had tripods for the heavy guns; the tripods were expected to arrive the afternoon of the inspection day. Fiske wrote that units were in their second week of training. His report on machine-gun units was dated a little more than a month before the division took over the Saint-Dié sector in Alsace, and three weeks later it went to the Argonne.

Apart from a lack of equipment for training were two other problems. One was that the field signal battalion was incompetent and could not train with the division. The purpose of the signal unit was to keep the division together, internally via telephone, cable, and wireless, and keep the division in touch with other units. Another divisional difficulty was the absence of the artillery brigade, which until mid-October was at an artillery camp in training with their new French guns, unavailable in the United States. For signals and artillery the division used substitute units, but this raised training difficulties once the division's units returned. Fortunately, in the case of the artillery brigade, it was excellently led, with no difficulties.[7]

After the Ninety-second completed its first-phase training, it entered, if ever so briefly, its second. This phase was to be in a quiet sector under Allied instruction. As the cantonment divisions began coming over in April and continued through early June, everyone was trained by the British. GHQ believed that the common language and heritage would make training easier. The British balked at taking the Ninety-second, and Pershing passed the division to the French. He properly reproached Field Marshal Sir Douglas Haig: "These Negroes are American citizens. . . . Naturally I cannot and will not discriminate against them."[8] The French were happy to have the Ninety-second and assigned it to a sector east and north of the town of Saint-Dié in Alsace.

The theory of phase 2 was excellent, if divisions followed it through. The training division would place units in the front line only under tutelage of an experienced commander. Training would extend to large units cautiously. All this required time. A period of twelve days was deemed necessary for a division to get into phase 2 with safety. At Saint-Dié everything seemed safe because of a lack of entry places by the enemy and control of almost everything by artillery.

Training by the French Eighty-seventh Division was a joke. The Ninety-second entered the sector on August 23 and completed entrance on August 31. It took over the sector on August 29. The French division was supposed to be out of the sector by September 5 but evidently used most of its twelve days of instruction to get itself out. The War College study concluded wryly that after the African Americans had the sector to themselves, the experience had "a certain training value."[9]

During the time the Ninety-second served in the Saint-Dié sector with or without the French, the happenings in the front line are difficult to be certain of, because division records are lists of what frontline troops were to study in their spare time. Topics were the same as what G-5 gave out to all divisions. Only one division memo of this training period survives, and it shows a certain greenness among the troops:

Our troops do not display sufficient activity and aggressive-
ness at night. This probably results from the fact that patrols
have justified the impression that to go outside our lines is to
insure being shot up by the enemy. . . . This must be changed.
Patrolling at night must be habitual, and if sentinels are not to
be trusted noncommissioned officers must stand over them
and see that friends are not fired on. Every sentinel must also
know that patrols are out and liable to pass this post or return
through it.[10]

It was during the division's first days in the sector that a sin-
gularly unfortunate event took place. It would have broken any
feeling among officers and men that at last, after their American
training, they were about to obtain instruction under foreign
officers who knew what was required for the division in a sector on its own. On the night of August 22–23, as the division
was passing under control of the French, a French colonel and
a nurse, Elizabeth Boursault, were riding in a carriage along a
road in the sector at Raon l'Etape, at half past midnight, when a
shot rang out that struck the nurse, mortally wounding her. Who
fired the shot was never determined. A soldier, Henry Williams,
of the 367th Regiment, was arrested and questioned. He had been
drunk and could not remember what if anything he had done.
General Pershing learned about this event, drove to the headquarters of General Ballou, and told the division commander he
would not tolerate such things and if there were one more incident—he had been hearing stories of rapes or attempted rapes
credited to the Ninety-second—he would break the division into
small pieces, sending the men home or turning its units into
labor troops.

Pershing rebuked Ballou in the presence of other officers, and
word of the threat by the commander in chief soon was out. One
of the individuals who heard Pershing was Brig. Gen. William H.
Hay of the 184th Brigade, who made it his business to inform all
officers of his brigade. He described what happened and the possible result beyond the shame it brought to the division, and said
he had known Pershing for thirty-five years and the commander of
the AEF would, if need be, do what he threatened.[11]

The entire situation displayed little thought by general officers. The killer of the nurse really was unknown. And the record of the division with women was excellent.

A final point about the Saint-Dié sector. The difficulty with the sector was not really the front line, which concerned the division command because of the willingness of sentries to shoot at anything, hence the possibility of shooting working parties of their own men. The difficulty in the sector was the Frapelle salient.

Not long before the Ninety-second came into Saint-Dié, its American predecessor division, the Fifth, attacked and took Frapelle from the Germans, showing the willingness of American divisions entering the line not to abide with the gentleman's agreement that prevailed between the French and Germans that neither would go beyond artillery dueling, machine gunning, sharpshooting, or occasional throwing of grenades. Then in a line that had lasted since 1914 the U.S. Fifth created the salient. Small units of German troops attacked the salient for four days in a series of raids, supported by heavy fire, tear gas, and sneeze gas. By that time the Ninety-second was in the sector and salient and had the task of repulsing the attacks and did so, suffering eight men killed, thirty-nine wounded, forty-five gassed. The French assisted with artillery and mortar fire.

In addition to holding Frapelle, the Ninety-second had the task of rearranging the salient's trench lines, no easy task. Taking a German position involved turning the arrangement of trenches upside down, for the first German line—a line usually had three trenches, the third being the point of resistance—became for the Americans the third. In case of artillery barrages the guns would fire on the first and second lines, and what troops might remain in them would take the fire as long as they could prior to retreating to the third line. With the German lines in American control, serious rebuilding was necessary. Wire and other barricades had to go up against German points of entry. It was necessary to build connecting trenches back to the second and third trenches. Last, the dugouts that had existed for German troops had to be replaced, for German artillery knew their locations. The old ones also had entries that faced north, which exposed them to artillery fire. The number of dugouts for each company subsector ran from fifteen to twenty, and they were of all sorts, depending on location and soil. The Fifth Division produced a plan for redoing the trench system that received the approbation of the French, and had begun to carry it out, but then left. The task fell on the 317th Engineer Regiment of the Ninety-second, together with such cooperation as came from French engineers.

At this juncture a question arose as to who in the Ninety-second would do the work, principally digging, as well as guard duty against fire or gas, while the 317th rearranged the system, including the dugouts. The 317th Engineers were uncertain about how industrious the infantry companies were, also how willing they were to get close to the line and encounter danger.[12] (More about this, linked with the issue of whether black company officers were effective, is discussed in chapter 3.) Certain it was that the Ninety-second's engineer regiment had a major problem on its hands with the Frapelle salient, bequeathed by the U.S. Fifth Division, and that, however the work was done, the problem was well in hand by the end of the short time the division was at Saint-Dié.

The white officers of the 317th made general comments about the unwillingness of the division's men to undertake patrols along the line of the sector, and those clearly were due to a misunderstanding of how the division conducted its patrols.[13] The truth appears to be that the division's infantrymen were not called upon to do much patrolling. One battalion commander in the 368th Regiment said that the patrols in his battalion were taken by the reconnaissance platoon of his battalion, not from men of the companies. The commander of the Second Battalion of the 368th, Maj. Max Elser, said that only once were his men called out to patrol. When that happened Elser did well with his troops, considering that they had had very little experience; they were green troops with little or no instruction from the French, and the result was not perfect but, all in all, did not show the poor morale mentioned by the 317th's critical officers. When called upon, Elser sent three patrols, one from each company on the battalion line. There was a marked difference in closeness of his battalion line to that of the Germans. The right was much nearer than any other portion, one hundred meters, the left four hundred meters. The patrol on the right went out and was attacked by machine guns—Elser believed it really was by riflemen using rifle grenades. The patrol commander, Lt. Frank Coleman, a good man, put his men in a dead place, probably a reverse slope, communicated with Elser, and worked his men out, excellent behavior on his part and that of the patrol. The second patrol went out in the middle and got into trouble. It received a barrage and was handled badly, eight men wounded, several seriously, one man missing. The left patrol did not gain contact and reported back with no casualties.[14]

After Saint-Dié the division entered the great battle of the Meuse-Argonne, assuredly a test of the Ninety-second's mettle. The battle opened on September 26, 1918, and lasted forty-seven days until the Armistice on November 11. It was by far the largest action of the AEF and the largest engagement of American forces in all of the nation's history, in any war, anywhere, with the largest losses. The U.S. Army forces in the Meuse-Argonne reached 1.3 million men; casualties—killed, wounded, and missing—rose to 100,000, of which deaths constituted 26,000. The next costliest battle in American history in deaths was Okinawa in 1945, where 13,000 men died, nearly half of them aboard ships supporting the operation.

That the Meuse-Argonne presented a challenge to the Ninety-second goes without saying. That in an account of the first of the division's two actions, which follows, the division's single infantry regiment in line, the 368th, together with two companies of the 351st Machine Gun Battalion, did not do spectacularly well might have been expected. That it did not do badly was better than many U.S. infantry regiments in 1917–1918. By no means was the attack in the Argonne a catastrophe, proof that African Americans could not and would not fight, proof of the racial theories of white supremacy so long prominent in the New World.

# TWO

# Argonne

IF ONE WERE TO HAVE ASKED the white field officers of the 368th Regiment what was wrong with the regiment after the infantry battalions, one thousand men each, came out of the Argonne Forest, the three battalion majors and the colonel commanding would have said: their African American company officers, captains and lieutenants, and their men. The white officers would not be expected to answer in this way. The division chief of staff, Col. Allen J. Greer, believed the 368th was the best infantry regiment in the division.[1] At the outset of the action the majors and their colonel may not have believed the chief of staff's remark, but they thought the regiment would do all right. At the end they could say, with truth, that the regiment had done as well as its French opposites, the 9th and 11th Cuirassiers on Foot. But they were terribly disappointed and in the case of the major commanding the Third Battalion outraged by what had happened.

The above analysis, to be sure, was nothing but racism, no analysis at all. It does not begin to analyze how the 368th got into trouble and how, eventually, it took its objective at the top of the subsector, the village of Binarville. At the end the plain fact was that the regiment succeeded, however embarrassing some of the episodes along the way.

The reason for the good result had explanation in the details of the action in the forest. What happened to the battalions divided into two phases as the men went forward and sometimes backward. The first, with preliminary explanation of arrival, the borders of the subsector, and its geography and man-made obstacles, saw the Second Battalion under Major Elser move out, and back, on the initial day of the attack, September 26. The next day, September 27, marked a joint attack of the Second and Third battalions, the latter under Maj. Benjamin F. Norris; the battalions divided the front line. At the end of that second day they seemed secure. The second phase of the 368th Regiment's experience in the Argonne opened with the event that labeled the regiment and the division and black officers and men as military failures—the disintegration of the two battalions. But there was more to the story than that. On the same day, September 28, the First Battalion under Maj. John N. Merrill went forward a short distance, came back to await the morning, and then moved up in earnest. The following day, September 30, at four o'clock, it entered Binarville, twenty minutes after the 9th Cuirassiers, and one company under Capt. H. G. Atwood went ahead to the northeast, where it spent the night.

## 1

The Ninety-second Division left Saint-Dié on September 21, and by train and truck and marching arrived in its assigned area as a reserve division for the American I Corps, holding the left line of the American Expeditionary Forces' First Army, on September 24. The division's 368th Infantry Regiment moved up that day to its subsector as part of a provisional brigade under the colonel of the 11th Cuirassiers. The regiments divided the subsector, French to the left of a line drawn between the village of Vienne-le-Château on the west, La Harazée on the east, both just above the Biesme River. The tiny stream meandered roughly east-west toward territory held by the French Fourth Army to the left of the line of the Meuse-Argonne (the lower half of the Argonne Forest eastward to the Meuse River). The subsector of Groupement Durand, the Franco-American provisional brigade, was to be a holding operation. The subsector moved north five kilometers into German terrain and for the Americans began with a width of approximately two kilometers and narrowed until at Binarville it was a half-kilometer. The theory behind the narrowing was that it would force the enemy to leave by having less and less territory in which to maneuver. By an alternative logic it was possible that the shrinking of an area of operations would favor the German defenders.

The latter had prepared positions to use rifle and machine-gun fire, and artillery received larger targets as troops concentrated in a smaller area (the kill zone).

The trouble with the American subsector was that French and German forces had been in it for four years and cut it up in small pieces. Generally the two trench systems, French and German, ran east and west. But parts of trenches wandered. Some had been kept up, others abandoned. To be sure that enemy troops would not come into their trenches, the two sides had erected barriers of barbed wire, everywhere anyone might presume to squeeze through. To make doubly sure, the sides emplaced crude but effective chevaux-de-frise, angle irons or spiked timbers strong with barbed wire, deadly affairs. In portions of the forested areas both sides had barbed wire, and men attempting to cross them would suddenly find themselves entangled. Artillery on both sides dug up the ground, meaning holes everywhere. To get through this morass, attacking or defending soldiers cut "boyaus," as they described them, or small pathways. The boyaus did not go forward or backward and could be traps as well as passages.[2]

Major Elser of the 368th's Second Battalion mentioned a further confusion in the subsector, which was that the Germans used tunnels between their trenches. On his battalion's third or fourth day a sniper fired from the rear. Elser told Lieutenant Coleman to take a man or himself back and stalk the sniper, and Coleman went back and killed him. Later the same day Elser thought another shot came from the trench ahead, and Coleman found a German officer behind a door to a tunnel and killed him. This was the first intimation of the underground tunnels. Elser did not get in the tunnels, but his men threw a grenade into one and closed it that way.[3]

To the far left of the American part of the subsector lay the Vienne-le-Château–Binarville road, the only decent road in the area. The tactics of the 368th tended to be to go up this road and then, upon halting, move off it, mostly to the right, sometimes, although it soon got into the French part of the subsector, to the left. There was a German narrow-gauge railroad far to the right, reachable only through trenches and boyaus and wire and chevaux. The farther the men moved to the right, the more the barriers: the French area was much less covered by obstacles.[4]

The road offered an advantage for moving troops, but it gave the German enemy an advantage if they chose to seize upon it, which once in a while they did. Their artillery to the north could close the road, shelling it. Here the 368th's adversaries missed an opportunity. They themselves were accustomed to using small-gauge railroads for transporting men and supplies and had little understanding of how the Americans employed roads. For the most part they left the road alone.

In equipment Elser's Second Battalion, and this would be true of the Third when it went into action, was poorly served by the French and by its parent organization, the Ninety-second. The Second had a company of heavy machine guns, a doubtful advantage because clearances were no more than twenty yards, not enough to use heavy guns. It had no light guns—no Chauchats. The obstacles, geographic and man-made, were so numerous that beyond going along the Binarville road it could take neither 34mm guns nor Stokes mortars. It had no *tromblons* (containers to hold rifle grenades) or French rifles with which to use them. For the most part it was equipped with American-made wire cutters, useless against heavy German wire; it had picked up a few heavy wire cutters but not nearly enough.

When Elser's Second Battalion moved out on the morning of September 26 everything had the appearance of order, no confusion. The men began on the Vienne-le-Château road, went north from the Finland trench, the first important German trench, thence to the Tirpitz trench, the second. The third was the Dromedary. Between Tirpitz and Dromedary lay the Moreau Valley; it was mostly to the left, in the area held by the 11th Cuirassiers, the regiment of Colonel Durand. Elser took the Second Battalion to the right into the Tirpitz trench, evidently allowing some men into the French subsector. His battalion did not reach the third principal German trench, Dromedary, just above the north side of the Moreau Valley. His men spread out through the boyaus, avoiding heaps of wire or chevaux.

The battalion commander chose to accompany half of his men, Companies E and H, as they moved off to the right into the Tirpitz trench, leaving Companies F and G to themselves, and this decision, separating himself physically, formed the first of his errors in command. It did have an advantage, in that he could deal with five hundred men, a sizable group, and assist their company commanders when he was, naturally, somewhat uncertain of their abilities. To attempt to lead the whole battalion personally would have been too much, especially in the cut-up terrain in which the battalion found itself. Still, the danger of losing the other two companies was evident, and in retrospect he should not have taken the chance. After the war when Colonel Rivers adjudged his performance he criticized Elser on this score, remarking that the other two battalion commanders did not directly accompany portions of their large forces and did not incur the danger of separating themselves.[5]

And with this decision to go forward Elser incurred another risk, his dependence on holding the battalion together through communicating with his rear headquarters via runners, no other means of communication being possible. The danger with runners was that the men entrusted with messages would lose them, perhaps on purpose, then claim they could not find the units to which they were going and thereupon turn up, a day or two later, safely in some place or other; for them there was no danger in roaming the virtual wilderness of obstacles in the advanced area. The officers in charge of battalion rear headquarters also appear not to have had careful instruction from Elser in regard to what messages to send up to him, and for that reason sent none, which was not at all helpful. After the action he mulled over this omission and did not seem to know what he should have done or they should have done.[6]

In direct touch with half of his battalion, and out of touch with his rear battalion headquarters, Elser took his men to the right along the Tirpitz trench until late afternoon when, suddenly, there was a chatter of machine guns on his right flank and the companies he was accompanying turned into chaos.[7] He had no chance to observe how far out the hostile fire was, nor whether from a single gun, heavy or light, or several guns. His men lost their wits and created a shambles, running, jumping into whatever depression or holes were available, otherwise falling flat; it was a regular tumult. He could not keep his eyes off the men nearest him. In that vicinity not a single officer sought to rally the men. He had been at the front of the troops and did not know what happened at the tail of the column. Not a shot was fired in opposition by any of the men.

He faced up to what he described as a slight move to the rear by cutting off fifty men trying to move back. He calculated there were three machine guns and no one hurt, and "hollered at them" to fire back, roughly a foot off the ground, and fire slowly. When words had no effect because the men were so excited, he shook or kicked them into attention. In many instances the men on the opposite side of the trail were firing between men on the other, and he stopped that. He thought the officers were beginning to take control.

He gave the order to cease fire so he could think about what to do. It was beginning to get dark, and he had to decide whether the men should stay where they were or move back. At this time an enemy plane swooped in and dropped a bomb that went off harmlessly. Desultory artillery fire began to come over the battalion in the form of shrapnel.

The question was what to do. The choice was whether to stay out in the trench overnight, which meant arranging the men, with suitable advance parties warning of further attack, or take the men back to the Finland trench, which they knew. The decision had to be made quickly, for it was getting late; this was September in the Argonne, the North of France where darkness came quickly in such country. Elser and his men had no large idea where they were, apart from general notions. The company officers had small-scale maps. Elser had had a 1:20,000 map, one inch equaling twenty thousand feet, but had given it little attention; after the war he told Rivers he could not remember what he had done with it, thought he had sent it back to his rear headquarters. He knew he had not gotten far enough to the right to come into contact with the 308th Infantry of the Seventy-seventh Division and could obtain no indication of what to do from them, that is, what sort of a line had been established against the enemy and where the enemy was, what lay behind the machine-gun fire that had upset his men. In deciding what to do, where to spend the night, Elser may have erred again in consulting his officers. It was his custom to consult; he sought that way to bridge any white-black difficulties. He had trained the battalion from its first days in the United States and was proud of what he considered its esprit, its willingness to work together. Unfortunately, he received divided counsel from the officers, who may have been discouraged by the melee over the machine gun or guns. They were as confused as Elser. It had been a long day, since five thirty in the morning. In the end confusion won out, and the battalion, what Elser possessed of it, headed back. He took the men slowly, no fast pace. The men at the other end of the front line, Company G and one platoon of Company F, came in too.

That left three platoons, a little short of two hundred men, to the left of the Tirpitz trench, close to the Binarville road. They were under Captain Jones and stayed out all night. Jones believed his men were under considerable machine-gun fire, and so reported, but unlike Elser and the others did not persuade himself it was so heavy, or threatened to be, to bring back the men to the Finland trench from whence they started.[8] So Jones and men stayed out at Hill 176 close to the road and the Tirpitz trench, acting as the left flank of the Second Battalion that, other than them, was not there.

Here, as the day of September 26 ended, something should be said about Elser and Colonel Brown, how Brown did not talk to the commander of his Second Battalion taking the men up to Tirpitz, to the effect that Elser under no circumstances should undertake to bring them down again at night, as Elser did. The reputation of the Ninety-second, not yet tested, even if Saint-Dié was more of a test (the lack of training from the French, the awkwardness of protecting the Frapelle salient) than it seemed. The approbation of Colonel Greer was perhaps in Brown's ears, even if he gave no indication of believing it. He himself had come to the regiment just before it went into Saint-Dié and did not have to prove himself, his ability to command, in any way that he might have drawn conclusions about. But too many questions were unsettled with the regiment, and it is difficult to avoid belief that the fault here was Brown's; he took his situation for granted until it was proved otherwise. Instead of attempting to calculate in his mind's eye what might shatter his regiment's, and the division's, fragile reputation in the minds of all the white officers, in and outside of the Ninety-second, seeing that any withdrawal would be defined as a retreat, conclusions drawn, he let things drift: he should have directed Elser, told him no backward movement whatsoever. It therefore is possible to conclude that the Second Battalion's movements, up and down, were Brown's fault, not Elser's, although by accompanying half his battalion and by losing touch with his rear headquarters, Elser had a good deal to do with the battalion's, and thereby the regiment's and division's, loss of reputation in the Argonne.

It is interesting that during and after the war nothing happened to Elser or Brown. The regiment had a lieutenant colonel while in the Argonne, Henry S. Terrell, whose duties seem to have been ill-defined. Terrell's movements were dim and unsubstantial. He disappeared, replaced by Elser, who was promoted perhaps for effort. Brown held his command until the end of the war, and kept his rank afterward, although many colonels were reduced. He was on the War Department staff in the mid-1920s, and might well have been kept there as a resident expert on African American officers and men.

Some of the success in the survival of these two officers was due to their literary ability, oral and written—they could set out what had befallen them and their units. Elser could wind himself up in words, evident in his almost garrulous after-action report about the Argonne and his testimony to the inspector, Colonel Rivers, in 1919. To Rivers he spoke for forty-three pages. The inspector was adept at asking the same important question in different form, but failed with Elser because of the latter's surprisingly detailed and in general interesting answers.

Colonel Brown was more crisp but had the ability to hold an outline and was able to advance pretty much what he wished to say, no easy talent. He had, the army would have said, the ability to command. Imagination was something else, and in failing to tell Elser not to come back made a large mistake, requiring the first day of a short action.[9]

September 27 marked a continuation of the Second Battalion's action in the Argonne, another movement up the road, but with the Third Battalion taking half of its line—that is, the two battalions each had lines of one kilometer. September 27 also marked, with the entrance of the Third Battalion, the appearance of a new commander, Major Norris, who possessed quite a different personality from those of Elser and Brown. The major of the Second Battalion and colonel of the regiment were Regular Army, both graduates of West Point. Norris in civilian life was a New York lawyer, a member of the firm of Bouvier and Beale. The firm's senior partner was the grandfather of a later first lady, Jacqueline Kennedy. Norris's command behavior partook something of the certainty of a New York lawyer. Perhaps it made up for his lack of experience in the field. He had been with the headquarters company of the 367th Infantry Regiment until September 4, in Saint-Dié, when he took over the Third Battalion of the 368th.

On the morning of September 27, in the Argonne, the 368th faced what seemed new tactics from those that obtained the day before when Elser's Second Battalion was in line—and so Major Norris had to face them as well as his first real experience in a big battle, the Meuse-Argonne. It started out, fortunately, with attention not on him but on Elser.

That morning, very early, a quarter to four, a message came to Colonel Brown from the brigade commander, Durand, that the 368th would employ new tactics, changing its mission from liaison to attack.[10] It is unclear if the change of words was important, but Brown believed it was. So did his battalion majors. It is entirely possible Durand mixed the two words unintentionally. In retrospect it does seem that even if the brigade commander saw some new tactic, presumably more aggressive behavior on behalf of his American regiment, the circumstances of the subsector held. This was the narrowing of the subsector from its base at Harazée-Vienne, two kilometers, to a half-kilometer at Binarville. The task of the American regiment remained more liaison than attack. The 368th had not found much opposition, at best a few machine guns. On Elser's left was Captain Jones's company on the end. Jones's principal achievement was staying up at the Tirpitz trench all night, unlike his commander. There thus was no reason to ask for more aggressive behavior.

Brown called a conference of his majors and there laid out Colonel Durand's supposed tactical change, also Durand's order for a move forward at a quarter past five. Under the best of circumstances there was insufficient time to order an attack. Brown's conference did not end until after the attack time. Durand's order asked for a two-battalion advance, impossible in a short time. Major Norris had brought his Third Battalion up behind Elser's jump-off line of the twenty-sixth, but it was necessary to move his two companies, F and G, out of the western portion of his own line. The brigade commander asked Brown to take his two battalions north to the German third-line trench, Dromedary, which meant going to the Tirpitz trench, passing through the Moreau Valley where the men, unlike the Tirpitz trench, had not been, and going on until a line that was one and one-half kilometers from Binarville. The French colonel commanding the provisional brigade was asking the Americans to work harder, a worthy request, but it needed an imprint of practicality. Americans under command of the French often believed their French commanders thought France had been in the war with enormous losses two and one-half years longer than the Americans, who could take a few casualties and be grateful for such advice as came their way.

At the conference Brown got into a tangle with Elser, who was tired from his long day on the twenty-sixth. There may also have been something to what Elser said. He told Brown his men were in "a muddled state," no condition to move over to provide room for Norris's battalion, and the better course was for Norris to have his men leapfrog Elser's rather than push them out of the western part of the line. Brown bristled at Elser's suggestion and flatly refused. The major made matters worse by asking that the new orders be put in writing, for Brown had given them orally. The inference was that Elser did not trust his own colonel. Brown refused.

Colonel Brown afterward believed Elser dragged his feet in getting his men to the new half-line side of the subsector. It was a matter of getting F and G over and making room for them. It took all morning, and at one juncture the colonel told his errant major, "For God's sake, Elser, get out and get your battalion on the way! H hour has already arrived."[11]

Elser's battalion did not cover itself with glory the second day. It went back over the territory it traversed on the twenty-sixth, that is, Finland up to Tirpitz. The major followed Company H, on the far right, and Company E was behind H. It is difficult to be sure what happened to the companies, as the major had not slept at all the night before and his personal account, in an after-action report and to the inspector the next year, is somewhat vague. He took with him a group of twenty men and sought to keep both companies going. He knew that H was getting into trouble, for his group began to encounter stragglers. He was nervous about the fact that H moved into an area containing trees, where men could easily become lost; the favorite excuse of stragglers was that they were lost. The two companies, H and E, did not get much farther than the Tirpitz trench and by midnight were back at the Finland trench.

On this second day Colonel Brown was more active than the day before.[12] Unsure what was happening, he moved his PC, his post of command, up to where he was a kilometer behind Elser. Late that afternoon he took out a reconnaissance group to find Companies H and E and determined that they were too far to the right, also too far apart. His group passed between the companies, he calculated. The area was unsafe for scattering forces, as Brown's group captured nine German soldiers and two machine guns.

It was two o'clock before Major Norris got his Third Battalion into the left of the regimental line and was ready to move forward, and its moves on the twenty-seventh were a little more impressive than those of Elser the day before, but not a great deal. He did precede his advance by a reconnaissance, something Elser had not done the day before, which was to Norris's credit; apparently it did not discover anything extraordinary, but at least Norris, who went forward with the group, knew what the battalion was going to encounter. The Third went forward by companies, I, K (the army did not use J), and M, with L following in reserve. He sent the companies up in a column of squads—eight men to a squad, eight squads to a platoon, four platoons to a company. Like the Second Battalion they used the Vienne-Binarville road. By nightfall they were beyond the Tirpitz trench, into the Moreau Valley, on the way to the principal German trench line, the Dromedary just north of the valley.

In the inspector general inquiry Colonel Rivers asked Norris, as he had Elser, if he maintained a command post easily identified by his companies. The answer was yes.

"How did your liaison work to your companies?"

"Very well, indeed. I was never too far away at any time to be out of touch with the exact position of my firing line."

"There was nobody on your firing line that was making any claim that he could not get in touch with you?"

"Absolutely not."[13]

Norris said he was unable to maintain communication with the Second Battalion on his right. He guessed, wrongly, at the reason, that Elser's battalion did not advance. Norris, unlike the approach by Elser, engaged in what one might describe as a know-it-all approach, all the way through his battalion's involvement in the Argonne. In comparison with the command approaches of Elser and Brown, it seems equally wrong. Elser was voluble and in his uncertain way more understanding of the Argonne's uncertainties, yet there was a kind of, to use Elser's own word about his battalion after its first day in the field, muddled way of command. One suspects the uncertainty was close to irresolution, and so communicated itself to his company commanders and other officers. Brown ignored details and took his role to be that of a director, giving instructions and relying on subordinates to carry them out. He was unhelpful in handling the details he could not easily remember, surprisingly insecure in his after-action report and a year later when talking with Colonel Rivers. Norris was something else. He handled his officers and through them their men. To one of his captains, although this was the testimony of the captain rather than Norris, his answer to a query was, "I am being paid to think for you. Join your company." His manner was altogether certain. He thus wrote out his after-action report and answered questions by Rivers. When in the field with his battalion on September 27, his first day, he had answers for all queries.

Norris's approach to his duties led into trouble with his accompanying French officers, whose tasks were to ensure such liaison as they could with the Cuirassiers to the left and help the Americans with tactical problems if they sought assistance.[14] On Norris's first day a question arose as to whether he should take his battalion to Dromedary on the other side of the Moreau Valley. He moved forward only at two o'clock, and as the day wore on he faced a choice, as had Elser the day before, of staying out overnight or going back to the Finland trench. Like Elser, Norris had no instructions, as he should have had, forbidding a return because of the possibility of adverse criticism by white officers outside the 368th Regiment. The Cuirassiers on the left, Norris knew, were keeping up with him. Durand had instructed Brown, who instructed Norris, to go north. As the afternoon advanced, the French officers, perhaps in accord with the tradition of French officers of taking positions in opposition to their own commanders, advised Norris to turn back, to

Finland. They also probably felt unsure of his judgment because of his certainty of what he knew. Norris refused. The officers said they would give no more advice and leave the battalion if necessary. Norris told them to go, which they did. He later discovered the Cuirassiers to the left had gone back to the Finland trench.

The experience with the French officers, having something to do with Norris's certainty, his command style, led to the first sign of panic within his battalion. Rivers asked Norris if there was any tendency of his men to panic and run from the line. The German defenders were more numerous than the day before, Norris noticed, judging from the slight opposition Elser had met. That was understandable, for the Germans had an opportunity to get forward and doubtless noticed the American tendency to move on the Binarville road. For the American moves of the second day there had been a slight artillery preparation throughout the night, by French 75mm guns, ineffective as one could have predicted because it was so thin. It did generate a slight enemy shell fire.

When Rivers asked Norris about panic in his companies, the answer was that from his post of command he saw panic in the reserve company, I. Its captain, C. A. Sandridge, had been with Norris during the argument with the French, and Norris admitted that anyone hearing it might have believed the officers correct, Norris inexperienced and wrong, presumably with Colonel Durand's goal of Dromedary equally wrong. Sandridge panicked along with his company, with everyone beginning to fall back. Norris went up on the road and met them, sending them forward again. He had no talk with Sandridge that night, and explained to Rivers that the captain had been an enlisted man with the 10th Cavalry for many years, commissioned at Des Moines, and naturally had an enlisted man's point of view. He was in ill health. He was not a strong character, Norris believed, and not qualified to be an officer.

The behavior of Sandridge might have been an omen for what Norris experienced the next day, but the major shrugged it off. And there was another that showed the weakness of K Company under a new commander, Captain Peaks. Something was wrong with K Company, and Norris does not seem to have understood it.

To show Norris's weakness as a battalion major, despite his certainty of the correct course of what he was doing, it is necessary to hear the story, which came out later, of Capt. Daniel Smith.[15] In mid-September in the Saint-Dié sector he shot a man who was moving around by himself in no-man's-land, and Norris put him in arrest; in this estate he accompanied K Company in the move to the Argonne. The company arrived September 24, and Smith did not go to a meeting called that afternoon by Norris for all officers. When Peaks returned from the meeting, Smith inquired what he should do, and Peaks said Norris told him that he could take Smith with him to the front or leave him behind. "I will not release him from arrest." Peaks left Smith to decide what he should do. Smith decided to go.

When the men moved up, Smith was put in command of a platoon. He was to take the platoon forward and report to Peaks. He received a guide. It was about two o'clock in the afternoon, the jump-off time. He went to look for Peaks and meanwhile saw many men roaming around Vienne-le-Château, all from Company K, and he asked Norris what to do with them and Norris said to take them forward and report to Peaks. He gathered them, ninety-nine, nearly half a company. Going forward, he went to where Peaks and K Company were supposed to be and found the captain gone, only a small group of twenty-nine men under command of 1st Lt. Azzie B. Koger. The lieutenant was ill and shortly left for the rear. This meant that Captain Smith was the only officer remaining and was in command of Koger's twenty-nine, his own platoon of some sixty, and the stragglers he found at Vienne, altogether a force of nearly two hundred.

Smith with all these men did well, by his testimony. He sought to find M Company at the left end of Norris's line but could not. He found I Company behind him. Halting his force, he went back and talked with Captain Green of I Company. The captain told him, "This is the damnedest balled-up thing I ever seen." They decided that Smith's virtual K Company would take the right of Norris's line and I Company the center, somewhere to the left. Where M Company was is not clear. Captain Smith said afterward he took his original platoon of K Company, despite being under arrest, up to the top of the north side of Moreau, meeting with little resistance.

The only difficulty with Captain Smith's story, as a second warning of unsettled conditions on the Third Battalion's front line, was that Norris did not believe a word of what Smith said. Norris stated, with his usual assurance, that Smith was not by himself with a scratch force, that he was always with other officers of Company K (six, said Norris) and commanded only a platoon of that company.

## 2

It was on September 28 that the Second and Third battalions of the 368th collapsed, for many reasons, involving the terrain, the artificial obstacles added to the geography, the command arrangement that passed orders from a French colonel to an American colonel, and the inexperience of the Americans. The last included the inadequacies of Colonel Brown, Majors Elser and Norris, the company commanders commissioned at Des Moines, and their lieutenants also commissioned there. It was a mélange of obstacles to success.

When the battalions collapsed on the twenty-eighth, the scene shifted to Major Merrill, a man of experience with Near Eastern and Far Eastern troops, a man also of intelligence and decision. But the battalion failures of the twenty-eighth stamped the 368th as an incompetent unit. Merrill tried, with unorthodox tactics, to redress this verdict, with what in a white unit would have been success, but his effort was too late for a black unit.

To understand Merrill's achievement, whatever its lack of appreciation, it is necessary to set out the collapses on the third day when Elser found he could not prevent his companies from going back, hence lost control of the Second Battalion. The men would not stay up on the firing line and came back individually or in groups, and so rapidly nothing could hold them. He remembered their coming back by individuals, squads, platoons, with officers moving to the rear on almost any explanation they could think of. He remembered watching the trail behind E Company and seeing Capt. Bob Thomas coming down alone. He met him by going up the trail to him after he had given him explicit orders to advance the company, not to move it to the rear, and no matter what happened he was to hold his place at least. Thomas told Elser that he could do nothing.

Elser managed to place a sort of line on the Finland trench—they had gone up to Tirpitz—and established a PC in back of Finland.

The collapse of the Second Battalion nearly broke Elser, as well as his line and battalion.[16] He was in a fragile personal state, so tense from the problems in the field he could not sleep either on the night of September 26–27 or on that of September 27–28. Colonel Rivers found out from Brown that after the Second's collapse Elser went back to Brown's PC and broke down and sobbed. He told Brown he had trained the Second and believed he knew the officers and men, and their collapse was the worst disappointment of his life. Brown said to the colonel he felt so sorry for the major he arranged for him to take a bunk in the PC, sending up his operations and intelligence officer, Capt. James T. Burns, as a replacement. Burns went up at five o'clock, he recalled, a half mile to the right of the Vienne-le-Château–Binarville road, and found only forty men of Elser's scout platoon; the companies had gone back. He stayed there all night and found none of the Second Battalion returning to enter his line, such as it was.[17]

On September 28 the Third Battalion collapsed, twice. It had come into line in the afternoon of September 27, having been in regimental reserve (at that time the First Battalion was in reserve for the First French Dismounted Cavalry Division). Norris on the twenty-eighth crossed the Tirpitz trench, the Moreau Valley, and reached Dromedary, with I, K, and M in line, L in reserve. The French battalion to the left was keeping pace. Then at noon the Third came under intense artillery fire, and the battalion broke, men and officers telling Norris they had received word to go back. Norris managed to stop the men and get them in approximate order. There was hope for a supporting artillery barrage, suggested by one of the officers. The major telephoned Brown, who asked the French for counterfire, the result being employment of four 75mm guns, this at three o'clock. The effect was hardly noticeable. The French infantry battalion, which had stopped, advised that it would start again at half past three. Brown called up and asked Norris to send his reserve company, L, to his right to help Elser. The company could not find anyone. At six Norris had a second stampede, the men going back as fast as they could in a disorderly mess led by the officers. In testimony in 1919, Brown said the terrain was so difficult it was impossible to control more than a platoon or two and Norris could gather only a remnant into an outpost line three hundred yards below Dromedary, withdrawing the balance of his men south of Moreau to Tirpitz, mount machine guns in what he considered the most advantageous positions, and hope for the best.

Brown's operations and intelligence officer, Captain Burns, had an explanation a year later that was less than appreciative of Norris, who despite Brown must have deserved at least part of the blame:

> Norris always claimed that his battalion was much superior to any other battalion, but nothing occurred; his battalion did nothing to demonstrate they were of different mettle. They had much less opposition, they had a narrower sector, they had the benefit of being in actual touch with the French on the left, and his battalion performed about the same as the others. They would make advance as long as there was no opposition and when there was opposition they would retire, and his men did retire and fall back that day, so that at the end of the day they were practically at the place they started from.[18]

As for what officers were involved in the second retreat, Rivers asked Norris, "The same officers . . . were engaged in this last retreat?"

"They were."

"What reasons or excuses did they give for the second retreat?"

"They gave the same excuse that some officer had ordered them to retire."[19]

With this low point in the fortunes of the 368th the scene shifted to the First Battalion under Merrill, who at the outset of the regiment's move forward in the Argonne on September 26 was at the bottom of the subsector.

Unlike his fellow majors and Colonel Brown, Merrill had all sorts of experience with troops. He began his career by enlisting for three years, 1899–1901, in the National Guard of Maine. For a few months in 1902 he was at West Point but quit and went to the Philippines, where he was in the engineers, cavalry, and constabulary—the last helping keep order during the Moro Rebellion and organization of the islands under American rule. In 1911 he went to

Persia, where with the rank of colonel he commanded from three hundred to two thousand men, in or about Teheran. For a short time he served as a captain under the British Indian Army commander Sir Percy Sykes. In 1917 he went back to France, thence to Texas to join a cavalry force, back to France and the AEF, until joining the Ninety-second. He commanded the First Battalion of the 368th beginning July 19, serving in the Vosges, and arrived in the Argonne on September 24.[20]

As reserve for the French division the First Battalion moved up into the subsector around noon on September 26, as Merrill remembered, under cover of forests all the way to Vienne, and the next morning, September 27, moved again to a position three hundred yards into the German line. This time the men were under full observation from sausage balloons over Binarville, two and one-half miles to the north. The men went forward two by two, in half platoons, separated by one hundred yards. The major put two companies in to the right, B and A, in the order named, two to the left, D and C, in the order named.

On the twenty-eighth, at three thirty, the First passed back under control of Brown, after the Second and Third showed signs of collapsing or were in the process of doing so. Durand assigned the First to Elser's location, and the portion of the line assigned to Norris went to a new French battalion from the 9th Cuirassiers sent to Durand by the commander of the First Dismounted Cavalry Division.

At nine thirty on the night of the twenty-eighth Merrill's First Battalion was on its way up the Vienne-Binarville road when it too encountered trouble. The head of the column began to stampede because of shelling.[21] This time—and what a change from the procedures of Elser and Norris—the First's major immediately, he was on the spot, took control. He struck several of the confused men full in the face with his fist, Persian and Indian tactics, and stopped the trouble at once, no talking or conferring or hesitation, after which he took position a hundred yards ahead of the column and the column moved on.

After this fracas the First did not go far before Merrill saw Major Norris limping down, and Norris told him of the "sheer impossibility" of relieving the Third Battalion, which had scattered. Merrill halted his battalion. He was replacing Elser, not Norris, but Norris said that he, Norris, had no battalion to the left of whatever line Elser then had. The front line of the 368th hence was wide open.

The road was muddy, the night dark, and this convinced Merrill to put his men on both sides of the road, and he and Norris went back to see Brown. There he met Elser, who spoke of "absolute hopelessness." Meanwhile, like Elser the day before, Merrill got into an argument with Brown, who wanted the First to take up some part of the line that night. Merrill refused, and Brown gave up, Merrill pulling his battalion back to where it had started that night, to stay until the next morning.

At Brown's PC, Merrill encountered the aide of the 368th's brigade commander, Gen. William H. Hay, and gave the aide a piece of his mind. "I was in a very angry mood, and told him I was going to tell him what I thought, and what we needed. I criticized very severely the lack of preparation in which we were in, and told him we had orders the next morning to proceed to the trenches. Merrill asked for fifty double-handle wire cutters, two machine-gun companies, a supply of grenades, a supply of pyrotechnics, and two 75mm field guns. He said he had none of these things and must have them."[22]

Merrill would never have described his demands of General Hay as blackmail, but his requests did possess a tincture of it. At that very moment the 368th's front line was wide open. The major of the First, with the only American force capable of doing anything to take the line, had just refused his own colonel's demand that he take it. Merrill was telling Hay that he could not move without equipment and gave Hay until morning (Hay, one might add, was to become a major general in the last weeks of the war and leave the Ninety-second).

The aide said he would go down in his automobile to brigade headquarters and do his utmost to get the equipment. With the exception of the field guns and a machine-gun company, he sent everything by four the next morning.

On September 29, at five in the morning, Brown went to Merrill and gave verbal orders for the First Battalion to move out at ten. According to Merrill he gave his orders "in a rather hazy manner," and the major would have none of them, insisting on written orders, as Elser had sought two days earlier. Brown told Merrill, "All right, you dictate the order and I will write it."[23] The major did so, Brown adding at the end that Merrill was to remain on the defensive.

One might remark, incidentally, that all this, as Merrill told it to the colonel of the Inspector General Department in 1919, was quite different from the after-action report of Brown and the latter's testimony in 1919.

The major then told his men what to do. He transmitted his orders orally to Capt. Vance H. Marchbanks and Captain Atwood and detailed his adjutant to give the captains the written orders and sent the adjutant personally to see that the battalion formed on the road at ten o'clock. At that time no one was on the road, and Merrill went personally and got the companies out, although this took three hours, until one o'clock. He began the march again with himself at the front of the column, companies in order, A, B, C, D. He dropped off D as reserve. At three he got the others into trenches two miles south of Binarville; the trench line was in the forest just above the Moreau Valley. He established relay posts for runners from each company to his PC and his own posts and runners to companies in case a company commander failed to keep in touch. He arranged liaison with the 308th Infantry. The Seventy-seventh Division was on the right, the Cuirassiers on the left. He put himself in a frontline dugout, No. 11.

After moving forward across the valley, Merrill the next morning, September 30, started the day with a personal reconnaissance, taking three or four men along with a French officer accompanying the battalion (unlike Norris, he was having no contentions with French officers, perhaps because he was fluent in French, but also one suspects because he was careful to weigh if not use their advice). They went to the left of the line and proceeded north for a thousand yards and found absolutely nothing, turned east and crossed practically the entire line and found no enemy of any sort. The French officers went still farther to the front, and it was clear. The group proceeded back about ten o'clock. That morning the French officer established liaison with the Cuirassiers to the left. Two or three patrols from the Seventy-seventh Division reached Merrill's PC. The major found it impossible to get his own officers to organize patrols and get them out to either side. He believed there was absolutely no difficulty in doing so and afterward told his officers what he and the French officer had done, made it clear that they could have done the same, and ordered an immediate advance north and sent word to Company D, in reserve, to move up. A written report went back to Brown concerning the new line.

When Merrill sent the report of the new line he told the colonel about a decision that he had just made. The decision was altogether typical of the major of the First Battalion. He said that he had the French on his left and the 308th Regiment of the Seventy-seventh Division on his right, and both groups were ahead of him—hence, his battalion was in a dangerous position where it was, in a pocket: the Germans could move down and attack. The reasoning sounded a little fabricated, but he gave it to Brown in knowledge that the latter could not do much, if anything, to stop him. His reasoning to the inspector a year later stressed necessity:

> Q: Do I understand rightly that when you started up the 29th, the French and the 77th American Division were about four kilometers in advance?
>
> A: No, sir, they were not. They were a little in advance of our left and right respectively, but on the morning of the 30th of September, unknown to me the French pushed forward as did the 77th Division. I considered that my position was an extremely dangerous one with the stability of the Allied lines, and my one purpose in going forward without orders, and which I had to do as my own judgment, was to save the situation and to straighten out the line.

And what did Merrill really have in mind in 1918? Delightfully he had told Brown that he had no orders: "I am not going to sit here uselessly, orders or no orders."[24]

One can safely say that Groupement Durand, and behind the composite brigade the French First Dismounted Cavalry and its corps, the French XXXVIII, did not want the Americans in Binarville. They had seen two American battalions fail and expected the same of the next, the First Battalion, and so at 12:35 a.m., September 30, Durand issued orders that the 9th Cuirassiers were to take Binarville, moving out at noon (and it was this movement that inspired Merrill).[25]

The orders said that the U.S. First Battalion was to stay at Tirpitz and perform the routine task of getting in touch with the 308th Regiment of the U.S. Seventy-seventh. Unfortunately for Durand, Merrill did not receive the orders until late that evening.

Merrill took the battalion forward at two o'clock that afternoon in three columns on a wide front—so if one column failed, the others would move. Their orders were to go as far as they could. The inspector asked if there was any objective. "Yes sir," was the answer. "I told them the objective was Binarville, and that I counted on them to get into Binarville ahead of the French."[26]

The tactics that followed called on the major's varied experience.[27] He told his men he would be behind them, and started each column. When in about twenty minutes the one to his left came abreast of his PC, he saw them stop. "I ordered them forward, and the order was not obeyed. I told them I would give them two or three minutes to move or I would open fire upon them." Nothing happened, and he fired two shots over the heads of machine gunners standing on a bluff in front of him. The men started. He went up the line, urging everyone forward. They all went ahead. He worked his way to the front, and seeing almost no officers, only two or three, the men halted in front of a clearing and claiming serious gunfire—there was some shell fire and machine-gun fire, but he could see no wounded. At this juncture he took all men within sight, Companies A, B, and C all mixed up, deployed them as skirmishers at intervals of five yards, and ordered them forward. They advanced two hundred yards and then fell flat. He ran into the line and got them going. It was as easy, or difficult, as that.

Merrill's men got into Binarville at four o'clock, twenty minutes after the French. Both forces moved back three hundred yards because of artillery fire and spent the night. Company A went two hundred yards above the village. At ten that night a message came from Durand that the American battalions—including what was left of the Second and Third—were to go to the bottom of the subsector, the first of the old French trenches, and reorganize. Merrill took his main force out at four in the morning, and Company A followed at seven.

On the field that afternoon and night, September 30–October 1, until the Americans left to return to the bottom of the subsector, relations between them and the Cuirassiers, with whom they held the village and environs, were entirely cordial. The French on the scene were not angry because Merrill's First Battalion had accompanied them into Binarville. The major explained himself in the tongue of the motherland. Captain Atwood told Colonel Rivers that when his company arrived above the village, his French opposite was most gracious. When Atwood offered cooperation he said, "Good, we would be glad to have you." Atwood had no machine guns and used twenty-eight or thirty French guns to guard his right flank. The two commanders put out combined listening posts. About this time Atwood's men used up all their food, and the French gave them bread.[28]

It is true, and the usual accounts of the 368th mention this, that the higher commanders of the French units during the attacks toward Binarville, notably the headquarters officers in the First Dismounted Cavalry Division, thought little of the value of the African American regiment, and whoever was keeping the division's daily operations report (*Compte-rendu des Evenements*) described the 368th's Second and Third battalions as "troupe absolument inutilisable pour le combat."[29] This was September 29, before Merrill showed them otherwise. The reason may have been that although the French were quite happy to have the Ninety-second in training in the Vosges rather than training under the British, they were not accustomed to having their own Algerian and Senegalese divisions officered by blacks—always the officers, of whatever rank, were white; even the noncommissioned officers were white. After the war, during the occupation of Germany, Merrill met Colonel Durand on the Rhine, and the colonel told him that in dealing with the 368th this was the problem. Interestingly, it had nothing to do with the cordiality at Binarville and of course said far more about French prejudice than American.

As mentioned at the beginning of the present chapter, when the 368th went out of the line in the Argonne, the field officers, the three majors and the colonel, were all convinced that African Americans required white officers. But the basic problem of command was the incompetence of white officers. It was of varying sorts, and one could argue that Brown, Elser, and Norris were commanders of some merit; their talents, unfortunately, did not work in combat and probably would not have worked with white infantrymen.

It could be argued that the poor training, at home and in France, the terrain in the Argonne, and the lack of equipment all had a part in the record of the Second and Third battalions. Merrill's experience over twenty years, and his personality, proved the main factor in the regiment's triumph. For the Ninety-second the action marked the division's first of two experiences in the U.S. Army's largest and most deadly battle from the Revolution to the present, and appeared to prove the belief of both Regular and temporary white officers in Pershing's forces that African Americans under black company officers were a prescription for failure. If the advance into Binarville under Merrill, together with later events in the division's history, proved otherwise, the judgment of the moment prevailed. It may have accounted for the army's refusal to organize African American divisions until late in World War II, not to mention include blacks and whites in the same units, until President Harry S. Truman's personal conversion to the by then pressing issue of civil rights, which together with the manpower shortage of the Korean War forced the army to mend its ways.

Colonel Brown reported casualties in five days as 2 officers killed, 2 severely wounded, 1 slightly wounded, 5 gassed; enlisted men 36 killed, 94 severely wounded, 87 slightly wounded, 45 gassed, 7 missing. Total casualties 279. The numbers gassed were reported by the men and could not have been correct; the Germans did not use poison gas against the Americans in the Argonne, and neither did the Americans against the Germans. The French on the American left used gas, and some of it might have drifted over the American part of the subsector. Emmett J. Scott's compilation of War Department and other materials—Scott was Secretary Baker's adviser on African American affairs—listed more than 450 men killed, wounded, and gassed. The final figures for casualties, published by the War Department in 1944, show 42 were killed, 16 died of wounds, and 222 were wounded between September 26 and October 7, for a total of 280. These figures do not include gas.[30]

The German opponents of the 368th, also the Cuirassiers, perhaps the 308th Regiment of the Seventy-seventh, were the 83rd Regiment of the Ninth Landwehr (territorial) Division and 254th

Regiment of the Seventy-sixth Reserve Division. In the general area between the U.S. I Corps and the French XXXVIII Corps, the Germans had two Landwehr divisions, with the Seventy-sixth put in between them on the night of September 25–26. Landwehr divisions were composed of older men and were second class or even third class. The Seventy-sixth had been brought back from the Russian front in March and was tired but gave a good account of itself in the Meuse-Argonne. German casualties are difficult to break out. Those caused by the 368th are indistinguishable from those caused by the Cuirassiers and the other regiments of the First Dismounted Cavalry and the 308th Regiment of the U.S. Seventy-seventh. The German Seventy-sixth Division reported 29 killed, 94 wounded, and 22 gassed.[31]

A crowd turned out at the Drake University Stadium to see the candidates of the Officers Training School perform, July 22, 1917. (John L. Thompson, *History and Views of the Colored Officers Training Camp*, State Historical Society of Iowa, Des Moines.)

Pillbox in the Argonne. Beside it is Lt. Col. J. Edward Cassidy, 317th Engineer Regiment, October 30, 1918. (III-Signal Corps 30577. All Signal Corps photographs are from the National Archives, College Park, Maryland.)

Maj. Gen. C. C. Ballou. (*Emmet J. Scott's Official History of the American Negro in the Great War.*)

Log road, 317th Engineer Regiment. (Album, box 15, Ninety-second Division historical, RG 120. All designations with Record Group numbers are from the National Archives.)

Putting in a standard-gauge railroad track, 317th Engineer Regiment. (Album, box 15, Ninety-second Division historical, entry 1241, RG 120.)

Perhaps the engineer, 317th Engineer Regiment. (Box 15, Ninety-second Division historical.)

Col. Earl Brown, Lieutenant Colonel Cassidy. (Album, box 15, Ninety-second Division historical, entry 1241, RG 120.)

Brig. Gen. John H. Sherburne in his office, Marbache sector, 167th Field Artillery Brigade. (lll- Signal Corps 44017.)

Mess line, 317th Supply Train, Belleville, October 12, 1918. (lll-Signal Crops 39550.)

"Big Nims" showing a problem with the standard gas mask, Third Battalion, 366th Infantry, Ainville, Vosges, August 8, 1918. (lll-Signal Corps 25930.)

Maj. Warner A. Ross, Second Battalion, 365th Infantry. (*My Colored Battalion*, frontispiece.)

Lt. Gen. Robert L. Bullard, Toul, October 28, 1918. (Ill-Signal Corps 31923.)

The commander-in-chief addressing the officers of the Ninety-second at the forwarding camp for the voyage home, near Le Mans, January 29, 1919. (Ill-Signal Corps 52537.)

# THREE

# Engineers and Artillery

IF ONE TOOK THE opinions of the three battalion commanders and the colonel commanding the 368th Infantry of the Ninety-second Division, it was evident that both black officers and black infantrymen failed in the Argonne. If, then, one took the opinions of the white officers in command of the 317th Engineer Regiment and the 167th Field Artillery Brigade of the division, it was evident that with white officers black troops in those specialties succeeded.

The engineers worked in the Argonne from September through November 1918, as the Ninety-second moved from sector to sector. In Saint-Dié they had cooperated with the French in ensuring the safety of the Frapelle salient once the Ninety-second's predecessor division, the U.S. Fifth, had taken it. In the Argonne the 317th Engineers initially worked on bridging the huge holes blown in the Route Nationale No. 46, the only good road for two of the I Corps's three divisions in line, together with removing the masses of barbed wire and chevaux-de-frise. For the rest of the regiment's time, until the end of the war (only Company E of the 317th went to the Marbache sector), the regiment devoted its attention to roads, under Lt. Col. J. Edward Cassidy, and narrow- and standard-gauge railroads under Col. Earl I. Brown.[1]

The 167th Field Artillery Brigade was in training in France until mid-October 1918—it could not train in the United States because of a lack of guns—going then to Marbache, where it showed its mettle, excellent support of the three infantry regiments in action there in the last days of the war, November 10–11. After the war the commanding brigadier wrote enthusiastically of how well his brigade handled itself, superior to other brigades in every way.[2]

What a relief the easy relationships of officers and men in the engineer and artillery units of the Ninety-second, compared with the complaints and hostilities of the division's infantry units! Almost no black civilians possessed the mathematical and technical training necessary for engineer and artillery officers. The war did not allow time to train such specialists. This was not a theory but a condition. It did not mean that the white officers in the Ninety-second's engineers and artillery were without racial prejudice, for they had plenty of it. In that regard they were no better than the average white American. It did mean that the engineer and artillery officers were technicians, from whose direction their units' drafted men had much to learn and thereby could accomplish their designated tasks.

According to the U.S. Army table of organization, engineer regiments were not nearly as large as infantry regiments. The latter comprised 4,000 men, an engineer regiment 1,500. When the 317th Engineers left the Saint-Dié sector for the I Corps just before the Meuse-Argonne battle opened, it consisted of 56 officers and 1,499 men; similarly, an artillery brigade was much smaller than an infantry brigade, the latter consisting of two infantry regiments together with auxiliary units. An artillery brigade had three regiments of about 1,000 men and officers each, with a total strength of about 4,000, that is, an infantry regiment, although commanded by a brigadier general.

# 1

In the case of the 317th Engineer Regiment of the Ninety-second Division—all infantry divisions in World War I whether in the United States or Europe had engineer regiments as inherent parts of the divisions—the immediate issue, upon formation of the regiment, was the need (said Engineer Corps officers) of white engineer officers. This contention dominated the choice of officers for the regiment from the very beginning of its existence. In the end the officers were all white except physicians, a dentist, and the chaplain. The men were random choices from the draft, none chosen for any engineering training, or experience.[3]

When the 317th formed at Camp Sherman in Ohio, the head-quarters of the Ninety-second at Camp Funston in Kansas assigned the necessary number of officers from the pool created by gradu-ates of Fort Des Moines, several captains and thirty-nine first and second lieutenants. At the same time three engineer officers, white, were assigned the 317th, Col. Earl I. Brown, Lt. Col. J. Edward Cassidy, and Maj. Clay Anderson. They constituted the only engi-neer officers in the regiment then at Sherman. In subsequent weeks and months the regiment was under the guidance of white field officers, the three mentioned above and African American com-pany officers, this being the makeup of the Ninety-second Division according to the War Department and in accord with the under-standing and approval of General Charles C. Ballou, the division commander.

The training needed supervision of the company commanders and especially of the lieutenants, of which there were five in each company. They could teach only what they knew. The men learned little about engineering. In this period down to and including the time they left Camp Sherman and, via Camp Upton, Long Island, took ship for Europe, the men became proficient in the science of military courtesy, target practice, and whatever else the African American officers learned at Fort Des Moines, but not much else, save their training by the black officers in such minor engineer-ing tasks as lashings and knot tying. Lieutenant Colonel Cassidy, the author of an excellent and quite large (126-page) history of the 317th, remarked that the enlisted men learned the knots but then, because the tying had no relation to anything, forgot them by the time they had gone overseas.[4] He was scornful of the infantry train-ing, because engineers, he wrote, were for other than infantry duty, even if on occasion they might have to go into the line. In the event, in France, the engineer regiments of several of the divisions went into the line, such as the First Division and notably the Thirty-fifth.[5]

Cassidy, the author of the regimental history, offered another reason African American officers were insufficient for the 317th Engineers, and this was their essential dishonesty. When the regi-ment was going across on the USS *Mount Vernon,* their transport, a black officer got into an argument with a sailor fireman and drew a pistol to make his point, and then lied when the near fracas was adjudicated. Cassidy said that a black officer would lie whenever necessary, that such officers had no understanding of the requirements of being an officer and a gentleman. He cited in support the inability of the 317th's black officers to keep their accounts straight. An officer's mess left five hundred dollars unpaid when the regiment mustered out after the war, and a similar sum came up missing in one of the company accounts. Under black captains the companies had no idea of pursuing what was obtainable upon request through army quartermaster stores and purchased such items on the open market. They kept no receipts and no lists of what they obtained.[6]

Colonel Cassidy probably had in mind the long history of the Engineer Corps, which during the nineteenth century was the principal corps in the U.S. Army. Of course, the corps in that time had no African American officers.

One suspects another factor in the belief of white engineer officers in the impossibility of African American engineer officers, and that was the remarkable rise in the importance of engineers in the generation or two before World War I. The United States became one of the leading industrial nations of the world. Engineering schools appeared, a notable one at Stanford University in California, where the young Herbert Hoover attended and learned the skills that took him into mining engineering and brought a reputation of "the great engineer" that after the war took him to headship of the Department of Commerce and then to the presidency. There was a professionalism among engineers not seen in the perhaps less celebrated and less skillful engineers of earlier decades, and it forbade creation of an engineer regiment such as the 317th composed of amateurs such as the Fort Des Moines officers.

What was happening came to the attention of Maj. Gen. W. M. Black, chief of the Engineer Corps, who spoke informally with the army chief of staff—this probably was Maj. Gen. Tasker H. Bliss, who was acting chief of staff in October 1917. He might have spoken with Maj. Gen. John Biddle, himself an engineer officer, who alternated in the office with Bliss. General Black thought he had an understanding about the 317th's officers, that they must, all of them, be white. Shortly afterward the field-grade officers were appointed, and he assumed the list of white company officers was omitted by mistake. Some weeks later he submitted a memorandum relating his assumption that company officers were white engineer officers and discovered to the contrary, an impossible situation if the 317th was to be more than an engineer regiment in name only.[7]

General Black was cognizant of an irrevocable fact, namely, that one could not make an engineer out of an infantry officer in the time that the regiment had before the division would go overseas, that a formula decided for the infantry would not work for engineers. And there was another factor that in itself seemed astonishing, and in retrospect appears astonishing, but Black said it was true. The Corps of Engineers needed approximately five thousand officers—it actually was a few less—commissioned from civilian life, what with the rapidly expanding army, and it received about fifteen thousand applicants, and among them was a single identifiable black. This was a Mr. Duke, who had graduated from the engineering school at Harvard University and had a minor post in the city government of Chicago. An army medical board examined Duke and found small physical defects that forbade his commissioning. Black believed that if he were commissioned anyway, this would weaken the medical requirements for engineer officers, but was inclined to waive them and give Duke a commission. Colonel Brown of the 317th believed that within the Ninety-second it would be possible to find a few black officers with rudiments of engineering, but had no officer in mind.[8]

At this juncture—by this time the infantry training of the men of the 317th had gone well, but the men knew little else—an inspecting Engineer Corps officer, Col. Lytle Brown (there were three Colonel Browns, Fred R., who would command the 368th Infantry; Earl I., commanding the 317th; and Lytle, the inspecting officer), offered a way out, which was to give the remaining black officers an engineering test. Col. Earl Brown had arranged for the appointment of white company commanders in place of the Des Moines commanders, persuading General Ballou to consult AEF GHQ in Chaumont, which concurred in their relief, and they left between April 15 and May 22, leaving the thirty-nine lieutenants. Lytle Brown gave the test on June 10 and obtained the result he and Earl Brown desired.

The questions were fair, but for anyone not an engineer officer they were rigorous:

Question No. 1: A flat-bottomed boat, with square ends and vertical sides, is eight feet wide and twenty-four feet long. Required: How much will the draft of this boat be increased by uniformly distributing a load of ten thousand pounds? (Weight of question 10).

Question No. 2: You have to build a trestle of sawn timber, which, in your judgment, will carry the trains of the Ninety-second Division. One bent of this bridge is twenty-four feet high. Required: A sketch of that bent, with dimensions of the members of the sketch and a bill of materials for the bent. (Weight of question 15).

Question No. 3: In the bridge of Question No. 2, what length of bay would you use? What are the dimensions of the stringers and how many are there in a bay? What thickness of flooring would you need? (Weight of question 10).

Question No. 4: Name the various kinds of road binders in use. What is water-based macadam? (Weight of question 10).

Question No. 5. Give two systems for mining galleries and shafts, that is, two systems for holding back and supporting the earth while driving galleries and shafts in mining. (Weight of question 10).

Question No. 6. You have to furnish water for a brigade of infantry of full strength in the front line troops. Required: the minimum amount of water you would furnish the entire brigade in twenty-four hours and show how you would arrive at the result. (Weight of the question 10).

Question No. 7. Show how you would find the distance from a point within our lines to a point behind the enemy's lines and tell what equipment you would ask for to do the work. The results must be accurate enough to determine the running of a mine gallery. (Weight of question 20).

Question No. 8. In a field bridge the strength in a simple tension member of mild steel of square cross section of the member is one hundred and fifty thousand pounds. Required: The size of the cross section of the member, all work to be shown. You may assume any quantities that are not given in the problem. (Weight of question 15).[9]

A passing grade was sixty. Two officers passed. The nine lowest were two at seven points, one at six, the rest zero. On the same day of the test Col. Earl Brown wrote Ballou asking relief of all black lieutenants, granted not long afterward, whereupon they left, replaced meanwhile by thirty-one white engineer lieutenants. In a report to the chief of engineers Col. Lytle Brown concluded: "Generally speaking, the company officers of this command are wholly unsuitable by education and experience to perform the ordinary field duties of engineer officers and it is certain that no amount of training, practicable during the present emergency, will render these officers fit to perform the duties which will certainly be required of them and upon the proper performance of which the effectiveness of the field work of the division will to some extent depend."[10]

The exchange of black Des Moines infantry lieutenants for white Engineer Corps lieutenants did not take place until the 317th was in France. When the black lieutenants left, they included the two lieutenants who had passed Col. Lytle Brown's test.

It was July 22, a month before entering the Saint-Dié sector, a long time after formation of the regiment at Sherman, before engineer training began. According to Lieutenant Colonel Cassidy, who was not a little prejudiced against the Des Moines officers, everything then "took on a new air, and progress in training was rapid." He avowed that "the enlisted men were highly pleased with getting white engineer officers, as they fully realized that the colored officers were out of place in the organization."[11]

There was some shortage of equipment. Upon arrival in France the division went first to the 11th Training Area, presuming it would find tools and engineer equipment.

The 11th had seen no American troops before, and nothing was available for training. Two weeks later a shipment of French engineering equipment arrived. It was necessary to share the shipment with four pioneer platoons, one for each of the division's infantry regiments. Cassidy estimated the 317th had 70 percent of its equipment—which considering the equipment of most U.S. Army units entering a combat zone was not at all unusual in midsummer 1918. When the 317th went to Saint-Dié it had to give back its escort wagons, which belonged to the Corps of Engineers and would go to the incoming units. This meant the 317th had to ask the division supply train for transportation of its own train equipment. Transportation, again, was at a premium for all units of divisions.

The Forty-second Division had to take wagons designed for carrying wounded and cut them down for use as supply wagons. The 317th had a hundred serviceable horses—horses and mules could not be brought over beginning in January 1918, because of the space they required aboard ship and the scarcity of shipping, even with British assistance; animals had to be purchased in Europe where prices were high and quality difficult because, in France, the French Army had taken the good animals. The 317th had six nearly unserviceable motor trucks, a motley collection that included models no longer familiar to American readers: Dennis, Karrier, A. E. Company, Riker. In addition, Cassidy wrote, with not much humor, there were two bicycles and a Winton motor car. But with division help the 317th made its way to the Saint-Dié sector.

## 2

The extraordinary success of the 317th Engineer Regiment, through its white officers (the officers believed), was evident in the missions it undertook and accomplished—and they were two in number, roads and railroads. Part of the road system of the I Corps was under control of—that is, kept in repair by—a detachment under Lieutenant Colonel Cassidy. This involved the road to La Harazée that ran parallel to the Biesme River at the bottom of the I Corps sector, and the road northward from La Four de Paris, the Route Nationale, north through Neuvilly and Boureuilles to Varennes and Apremont. Colonel Brown had the railroads, light and standard gauge.

The division of tasks occurred on October 5. This was the day after another arrangement, involving three battalions of infantry from the Ninety-second employed as laborers, came to an end with the departure of the division for the Marbache sector. The laborer arrangement did not go very well, understandable because there were not enough picks and shovels to keep the infantrymen busy, also because they were not happy with their new duties instead of serving in the line. Their supervision may have been inadequate. Col. J. A. Baer of the Inspector General Department thought it was necessary to assign tasks and prevent troops who failed in their assignments from eating, an interesting proposal. He estimated the efficiency of the infantry at roadwork as 40 percent. When the arrangement came to an end, there were no laments, and the decision of the I Corps engineer for the 317th seemed much more sensible, with engineers in charge of what was an engineering task.[12]

Keeping the roads in shape in wet weather was a special difficulty, for the 317th had only four trucks for use of the entire regiment and the road detachments had to use local stone. Just a few inches under the ground was that stone, and it unfortunately was argillaceous sandstone; this meant it was wonderful for German machine-gun or artillery emplacements, for pits for the guns required no revetting, the stone capable of easy cutting with tools. As road filler it was far too soft, and under the wheels of trucks or wagons it ground down in two days, requiring new fill almost as quickly as the old turned into mud. The Meuse-Argonne, in northern France, was lashed with autumn rains, and that meant mud everywhere.

Cassidy did what he could to fill the roads, and one recourse was to blow up the German concrete pillboxes and use the pieces. The men put in timbers along the sides of roads and stabilized them with German iron pieces, and cut down the unduly high crowns of roads and put that fill to the sides next to the supported timbers.

As soon as Cassidy could, and the idea probably occurred sooner but it was possible to carry out only on October 5, he sought to acquire good stone in place of the argillaceous, but this lacked the support of a captain who controlled the twenty-four trucks the 317th obtained from the First Army. The arrangement was to ship stone to Les Islettes and truck it north on the Route Nationale ten or twelve miles to where it was needed. The trucks had to vie for position and proceed with undue slowness in the stream of traffic constantly on the road, and it seemed that even with this handicap the operation would work. Instead, a certain Captain Weir of the I Corps engineers undercut what Cassidy arranged. Why Weir did this Cassidy did not know. One day he reported to Cassidy seventy-six truckloads of stone delivered whereas twenty-three loads were delivered. Other days but fifteen to twenty truckloads were received when forty to sixty were reported.

In addition to repairing the roads with native stone and then failing the stone that Captain Weir did not deliver there was a need

to widen the Route Nationale from Varennes to Apremont, to provide for two-way traffic. In peacetime the fine macadam Route
46 accommodated carriages, and wagons could get to the side to
allow two-way passage. With the big-bodied military trucks this
was impossible. What with the difficulties of keeping the road in
order above discussed, widening was a formidable task. Cassidy
undertook it and gradually, as days and weeks passed, managed
it in crucial sections.The difficulties under which the 317th worked
when dealing with roads were compounded by the misconduct
on the roads by varied units of the divisions—something Cassidy
could not handle unless himself present at the moment of commission. Here the fault in part was a lack of presence of high-ranking
military police. Usually, the police on duty were privates or corporals, sometimes they themselves knew little of the rules they were
to enforce, and in any event it was easy for a ranking officer to
face them down, despite what the policemen had to say. On the
other side of the sector of the I Corps along a road affecting the V
Corps and III Corps, two full colonels did this with impunity. At
night when identities were uncertain, low-ranking officers could
act similarly.

The result was that units parked their vehicles or wagons on
roads, as it was convenient and their commanders, colonels or
even brigadier generals, were close at hand. On one occasion an
entire artillery brigade with all trains went into the Argonne without concise orders as to the route northward. The column halted for
two hours, blocking the road, occupying five miles, while requests
for orders about the route they should follow went back to division headquarters. In the early days of the advance the motorized
machine-gun battalion of the Seventy-seventh Division received
an order to halt on a road, did so, and stayed there three days,
blocking a third of the road to both traffic and work and turning
a two-way road into a one-way. Parking on this road was forbid-
den by corps order. On November 3 a long ammunition train of
the V Corps started west on a road from Landres-et-Saint-Georges
just before dark, and halfway to Saint-Juvin came on a mule train
going east, against orders, for the road was one-way west. The
truck train ditched itself trying to keep from running into the mule
train. Cassidy encountered this mess and ordered the mule train

ditched. It turned out that the military policeman, a private, had informed the officer of the wagon train that the officer was going against orders but the train officer went ahead anyway.

Cassidy's roadwork involved a great deal of labor pulling trucks out that had gotten off the road. This often involved overloaded trucks with ammunition, this because of the shortage of transportation. His men had to unload as many as 115 ninety-pound shells for 155mm artillery pieces before pulling trucks out; a three-and-a-half-ton truck with this load was 100 percent overloaded.

Part of the trouble with ditched trucks was the nature of the trucks. The four-wheel-drive truck was the worst, the steering mechanism broken. Such a truck also was top heavy. The high steel body of an ammunition truck was especially bad, subject to ditching. The heavy Mack trucks were good on dry roads, but because of their weight would dig in quicker than almost any other make. Many of the trucks did not have jacks or towlines. Colonel Cassidy kept a block and tackle in his car and one afternoon pulled out, within two hours, twenty trucks. The latter had ditched themselves on both sides of the road, tying up traffic.

As a professional engineer Cassidy easily saw the military utility of the Caterpillar tractor, which army officers before the war had virtually ignored. On the night of November 2, the fourth and highly successful AEF attack in the Meuse-Argonne was moving forward rapidly, and every member of the army in northern France was exuberantly taking whatever measures would keep up the momentum, for the end of the war, so difficult to see prior to this time, was looming as a possibility. Traffic conditions on the Saint-Juvin–Landres-et-Saint-Georges road were bad. There was rain and mud, and the narrow roads and darkness were playing havoc with truck trains. Cassidy's men, with his full participation, "borrowed" a couple of Holt Caterpillar tractors from two heavy French gun crews that had parked them for the night and were paying no attention to them. The 317th Engineers ran them all night, producing "great results" in keeping the traffic moving. The regiment's men then brought the Holts back, "and it is quite possible that the disappearance of gasoline in their tanks has been laid to evaporation."[13]

All the while that detachments of the 317th were bringing order out of the roads of the I Corps and the traffic they were carrying, a detachment under Colonel Brown was at work on the railroads, both the sixty-centimeter, or small-gauge, lines and the standard-gauge lines. And like the work of Cassidy and his men on the roads, the railroad detachment was every bit as successful, impressively so.

An efficient officer, as much as was Cassidy, Colonel Brown divided his railroad men into groups, and each had a section of the task, geographically defined. They did not have to move around, wasting time getting from one place to another. When each rail group finished the work on narrow-gauge lines in their area, they turned to standard-gauge lines.

Cassidy's history relates that in the work on railroads the 317th suffered from a lack of cooperation with the railroad engineers of the First Army, who were not officers of the Engineer Corps but civilians taken from railroads in the United States, turned into officers by giving them, he wrote, uniforms. They lacked the practicality of corps engineers. They suffered, Cassidy wrote, from having a single thought in mind, to obtain credit for anything they did.

Here Cassidy, a Regular officer, may well have been unfair, for the U.S. Army in World War I was essentially a civilian army, its successes caused by the presence of civilians. Some ranking officers, such as Brig. Gen. Charles G. Dawes, later vice president of the United States and ambassador to Great Britain, performed in the AEF with wondrous efficiency. The truth may have been that Cassidy and Colonel Brown did not like the raising of a civilian to a rank that was above theirs.

The initial disagreement between Brown and Cassidy, on the one side, and the railroad engineers, on the other, was over the possibility of combining the French and German light railway systems. The railroad engineers believed it was impossible because of the difference in grades. What bothered the civilians may have been the amateurish way in which German engineers ran the tracks of their sixty-centimeter rails—helter-skelter, without reconnaissance. In a word it was unprofessional. There were many switchbacks, which impressed the 317th's officers as a simple starting out in the general direction of where they wished their lines to go and then getting there any way that suited their fancy.

The fact, however, was indisputable that the small-gauge lines were efficient. The German system was complete, branch lines laid up to the rear of battalion sectors. In the case of artillery, shells were delivered directly to batteries and in many cases directly to individual guns. Especially was the latter true of guns of larger caliber.

A reconnaissance by the 317th showed that it was feasible to connect the French and German sixty-centimeter lines, with only two miles of new line necessary. There was difficulty in construction of the new line, for it had to run through French and German trench lines and, in addition, no-man's-land, where every sort of obstacle existed, "a tortured stretch of ground" full of shell and mine craters. The regiment was up to the task and in the Argonne on October 15 made a connection between the top of the French line at the southern edge of the forest at Maison Forestre and was sending up 120 to 200 tons of freight daily as far north as Senuc. By late October much ammunition was going up, for 75s that were the staple of American artillery brigades, also the 9.2 howitzer shells for the 155s. The latter were gas shells for the massive gas attack by AEF artillery on German machine guns above Grandpré in the Bois des Loges and enemy artillery batteries, nine of them, in the Bois de Bourgogne opposite and above the Bois des Loges. This gas attack, employing forty-two tons of gas on October 29, 30, and 31, broke the German resistance in the I Corps sector during the AEF attack of November 1–2.[14]

Once the French and German lines were connected, the 317th found itself again in opposition to the ideas or, if not that, the behavior of the professional railroaders at First Army headquarters, the uniformed civilians. This time it was an argument over railroad engines, which the 317th lost, for the First Army experts possessed the engines. Altogether the 317th Regiment possessed a few gas engines and a single steam engine. If the regiment had had more engines, as Cassidy wrote, it could have sent forward to the advanced lines each day the equivalent load of two hundred motor trucks, in addition to what it was delivering.

In addition to the problems of constructing sixty-centimeter lines across the French and German trench lines and through no-man's-land, the regiment had to deal increasingly with German destruction as the lines went north. In the line from Sivry to Buzancy the enemy blew twenty-one mine craters, fifteen to eighteen feet in diameter and eight to ten feet deep on an eight-foot fill. The men had to find and transport new fill, not easy to do, in addition to making right all the German-arranged chaos. By November 1 the Argonne, up to Grandpré, had its efficient sixty-centimeter lines. Between that time, despite the destruction, and the end of the war, the men of the regiment opened a narrow-gauge line to Buzancy. By this time the wonderfully efficient regiment was making a reconnaissance to extend the line to the top of the entire Meuse-Argonne sector, the vital German double-track rail line at Sedan, the very goal of the AEF during its last attack against the defending Germans.

The other portion of the 317th's railroading work, not as spectacular as construction of sixty-centimeter lines or their reconstruction, was making standard-gauge lines usable, trackage the German Army developed during its four-year residence in the Meuse-Argonne area. The line to which Colonel Brown gave attention was that from Apremont—it was a double track—to Grandpré, from which a branch turned east to Saint-Juvin and then (single track) north to Buzancy. Here there were two enemy measures against the Americans, one of which required ordinary, if difficult, engineer construction. This was the blowing up of piers and abutments across the Aire and the Aisne rivers. Colonel Brown estimated the damage as minor and reparable. The damage to the girders was something else, for they would need replacement. The other problem needing attention was damage to the rails of the standard-gauge line, which was considerable.

This rail problem in reconstruction was large but possible of solution, with one piece of inventiveness or another. The one was workable only on the rails not destroyed, and more easily on double-track lines than single. It was to turn such tracks into single tracks by taking what unblown rails were available and substituting them. Fortunately, the line of double track had sufficient rails to do this.

The single-track portion of the spur line north from Saint-Juvin was something else. Here the enemy had placed a charge under every other rail, and the explosion sheered off two feet on each side of the fish plate, taking the latter as well as destroying the rails. Or so they seemed. Brown noticed that the rails were of good hard steel and the breaks were straight, not in fragments. He had on hand a supply of fish plates and spikes. What he needed was one or two acetylene torches with which to cut the rails clean at the breaks, and then it would be simply a job of boring holes for the plates. But he had no such torches, and if First Army railroad officials had them they said nothing about them. The Saint-Juvin–Buzancy line was fourteen kilometers long, and there was not much to be done about it.

**3**

As for the 167th Field Artillery Brigade, it was every bit as well handled, if also with white officers, as was the 317th Engineers. Its performance showed that African Americans were as fully capable of accomplishing the missions of artillery as they were of engineering. In the instance of artillery, the moving spirit was a civilian engineer, not a Regular officer.

In the arrangement for the 167th Field Artillery Brigade to rid itself of all black officers, save for a physician, dentist, and chaplain, that is, transferring to infantry units the Des Moines officers, which happened in France, there does not seem to have been any definite process as in the 317th Engineer Regiment. There was no detailed consultation with careful weighing of courses of action. The reason for transferring the Des Moines officers, bringing in white artillery officers, may have been the obviously technical nature of the brigade, the 149th and 150th regiments each with twenty-four 75mm guns, the 151st Regiment with twenty-four 155mm howitzers. Finding officers among qualified white civilians was fairly easy. It was something else to discover qualified African Americans.

For several months the 167th was officered by African Americans, graduates of the Des Moines Officer Training School, who almost obviously could not handle the technicalities of artillery. They taught what they knew, the School of the Soldier, the rudiments of army discipline. By all testimony the artillery regiments of the brigade under the Des Moines–trained officers appeared military in deportment.

The brigade's regiments knew almost nothing about firing guns and howitzers because they did not possess any beyond a single battery, four guns, of the Old Army's light pieces known as the .02

(for the year of its issue). The army decided that its artillery units would use French pieces, and this meant waiting until the units arrived in France. There it received the guns and howitzers, learned their mechanics, and fired them on French ranges.

There was an attempt to send Fort Des Moines–trained officers to artillery school, but it proved of no avail. Two dozen were sent to the army's School of Fire at Fort Sill in Oklahoma. There they received every opportunity, with no prejudice over their color, but from the outset the tuition for the most part failed to take. At the very beginning officers failed the entrance test. Week after week contingents left, going back to Camp Dix. In the end six officers made it through the course and were commissioned to the artillery before going east to their units. One more effort was made to train the Fort Des Moines officers. About May 1 a troop went to the Officer Training School, Artillery Section, Camp Meade. In about a week they returned to their regiments.[15]

All the while the regiments at Dix were as well equipped as other regiments around the country, which was not saying too much, for American industry had difficulty even producing ordinary equipment when the army brought National Guard and draft men into the cantonment camps in October 1917. This, again, as had other factors above related, interfered with the training of the artillery brigade. An inspector remarked that one of the regiments had rifles but for 60 percent of its men had no revolvers and pistols, no machine guns, eight trench mortars, 60 percent bayonets, 35 percent scabbards for them, and everyone (said the inspector) had mess kits. All of this meant that even for ordinary infantry training, the regiments hardly had enough equipment. The 349th and 350th regiments, incidentally, had no signal equipment, essential in artillery work (even if there was only the single battery of .02 guns).[16]

It was little wonder that during the seven months of training in the United States the artillery brigade was getting nowhere. The inspectors were not encouraging. One of them wrote that the regimental commanders were not hopeful of making anything out of the units. The commanders blamed the African American officers and men who on account of lack of education and, they added as if the two factors were the same, lack of intelligence were almost hopeless as artillerymen. "In my opinion," said this perhaps biased inspector, "it will take at least a year to train these regiments so that they can be sent to the front."[17]

Another factor affecting the training of the regiments, although this was common in almost all divisions going overseas, was the infusion of large numbers of new men just before the Ninety-second left the United States. The 349th Field Artillery Regiment had trained with an average of four hundred men, far below table-of-organization strength, and in June 1918 raised its numbers to nineteen hundred by receiving raw recruits with no training relating to artillery work.[18]

Upon reaching France, the brigade was stationed in two places, Montmorillon and Lathus, and came together at La Courtine for artillery training. By this time it was August 1. In the latter part of October the brigade arrived at the Marbache sector.

But something happened in August that turned the 167th from an organization of no promise into a first-class unit, and it seems to have been a result of two dramatic changes. One was obvious. This was arrival of the brigade's guns, suddenly, about August 1. It was not all of them, for in addition to a full complement of 75s there was only a single battery of 155s. It was enough, though, and the brigade undertook a full schedule of training in the drill regulations. This was a completely different experience from the theoretical training of the preceding weeks and months, back to the brigade's formation at Camp Dix.

The other change became evident only after the war when the General Staff College asked the commanding general of the brigade, Brig. Gen. John H. Sherburne, to bring together his memories of training.[19] This new officer who came to his command only in midsummer wrote frankly and, one must say, extremely well (he wrote with admirable style) about how he put the brigade together, made a silk purse out of the sow's ear he thought he had received. "I came to the brigade with the feeling that it was an impossibility to make artillery out of colored troops," he confessed.[20] Instead, he produced a superb brigade.

General Sherburne was not a Regular officer but brought in as a civilian engineer. He had a considerable background, and his office was at 53 State Street, Boston. Once he discovered the possibilities in his brigade he took command with what might be described as the confidence of a Bostonian. He scattered all the brigade's confusions in a bare twelve days, until it went to La Courtine on August 12. "The enlisted men [draftees—the army chose to describe them as enlisted men] worked with a zeal I have never seen equaled, and while slow to learn, appeared to be fully as accurate in their final work as were white artillery personnel. Competitive tests given to the regiments at the end of ten-day training were excellent both in accuracy and speed." The average AEF battery at the front fired three or four rounds a minute, for 75s, and frequently fewer. The top speed of a 75 was thirty rounds, almost never equaled. The present writer knows only of a battery in the Thirty-fifth Division's brigade, not the battery of Capt. Harry S. Truman, that on one occasion when the battery commander thought, mistakenly it turned out, the division was threatened with collapse managed twenty rounds. One gun crew of the Ninety-second's brigade fired four rounds in six and two-fifths seconds. Another made four in seven and a half.[21]

Sherburne said he would have compared his brigade to any white brigade in the AEF, if his men had had a little more experience. The general's judgment was corroborated by an African American writer, Charles H. Williams, sponsored by the Federal Council of Churches to investigate the achievements or failures of black troops. He related how a French artillery officer arrived to test a barrage laid down by the 150th Regiment, one of the 167th's light regiments, and after it completed the fire mission jumped up and clapped his hands, saying it was the fastest and most accurate he had ever seen.[22]

When Sherburne wished, he could show his civilian side, not always in diplomatic ways, and like many National Guard and Reserve officers he could take his spleen out on Regulars. His three regimental colonels were Regulars. He believed that the U.S. Military Academy was a little, irrelevant school somewhere along the Hudson. The general said that he, Sherburne, was out to crucify Regulars. One of his colonels heard him say this and that when he got through with a Regular, the WP after the latter's name would resemble the IQ marked on a horse waiting to be disposed of.

On October 26 Sherburne visited the artillery brigadier of the neighboring Seventh Division, to the left of the Ninety-second in the line of the Second Army; the two brigadiers needed to concert their artillery plans in the event of attack. Conversation seems to have been comfortable enough. The Seventh Division's artillery brigade commander had received a communication from the Second Army ordering the relief of units of the 19th F. A. Regiment by units of Sherburne's 149th. The latter was commanded by Col. Dan T. Moore. Several hours later Moore and two officers went to the PC of Colonel Dunn, commanding the 19th, and there learned the orders from the Second Army. After giving orders for the replacement, Moore went to Sherburne's headquarters. Some hours had elapsed in the course of which Sherburne had said nothing to Moore about the orders sent down from the Second Army.[23]

All this seems harmless enough—it was quite possible that General Sherburne had not yet received the word from the Second Army to send units of Moore's regiment to replace the troops of Dunn, or if he had received the orders felt there was no immediate reason to make the replacement and had not bothered to apprise Moore. The latter somehow took offense at what appeared to him a dereliction of duty on Sherburne's part and made a complaint to the inspector general of the Ninety-second, Lt. Col. H. P. Harbold, asking for the general's relief because of an inability to command. All three of Sherburne's regimental colonels spoke against him, and the issue went to General Ballou, who agreed with them and sent the dossier about Sherburne to the Second Army.

On November 20, after the war, Ballou sent a long exegesis to General Pershing about his own treatment by the Second Army, in particular by its commander, Lt. Gen. Robert L. Bullard, and in the course of it added another criticism, beyond that advanced by Sherburne's colonels, to the dossier accumulating about his artillery commander. When the Ninety-second was preparing to attack on November 10–11, Ballou had asked Sherburne when the 167th Field Artillery could support the 183rd Infantry Brigade in a general attack east of the Moselle. The 183rd's commander, Brig. Gen. Malvern Hill Barnum, would send preliminary forces early on the morning of November 10 and later that same day his main force and needed artillery support for the latter. Sherburne said he could not support Barnum until four o'clock. Ballou told Pershing that he, the division commander, was outraged, for Sherburne's lack of cooperation would throw the main attack too far toward the end of the day and hence limit it. Barnum, it turned out, could not himself attack until four o'clock, but this made no difference; Ballou did not mention that point and advanced his contention against Sherburne.[24]

During the testimony in the Sherburne investigation the probable real reasons for his colonels' and Ballou's discontent came out. One was the West Point allegations. The other was Sherburne's ability to turn a fourth-rate organization around in a few days. Meanwhile, Brig. Gen. William Lassiter, artillery commander of the Second Army, informed Ballou that Sherburne was difficult but highly competent.

In General Sherburne's postwar appraisal of his brigade he offered an account of African Americans worth remembering. He said that the average black artillerist was slow to learn but hardworking in an inspiring way. The typical soldier, he wrote, was accurate with his hands, once he learned the techniques of sights and instruments. In motor mechanics, he noticed, both in handling the tractors of the 155mm howitzers and in driving trucks, the black artillerists were, in his opinion, fully as good if not better than their white opposites. Until the arrival of the tractors, the brigade did not have sufficient animal transport, and Sherburne could not forget how the men pitched in and did what needed to be done, turning themselves into quarter-horsepower prime movers. On October 19 when the two light regiments moved from Toul to the Marbache sector, they discovered upon arrival that they lacked transport; the men moved the 75s into position. On October 31 men of the heavy regiment moved all six of its batteries by hand at night over a distance of one-half to one-and-one-half kilometers. As for morale under fire, Sherburne watched the brigade under fire and never saw a lack of courage.[25]

It was General Sherburne's feeling that the men, if properly led, were equal to any task to which he set them. The leadership of the noncommissioned officers was excellent—he evidently had no trouble finding men capable of being noncommissioned officers, after inspectors and the colonels of the regiments said African American draft men were too uneducated and of too low intelligence to provide a sufficient cadre of noncommissioned officers. He saw more than a few noncoms who were quite capable of being officers but in talking with them learned that the best men were frank in saying that they preferred to remain in the ranks because of the hostility of their own men toward black officers. "In conclusion, I would say that such efficiency as the brigade obtained was principally due to the splendid service of the white officers. The enlisted personnel were plastic, and it was possible to mold it speedily and effectively."[26]

# FOUR

# Marbache

IN THE MARBACHE SECTOR of the American line in France, where the Ninety-second Division spent the last month of its wartime service with the AEF, the African American company-grade officers leading African American troops did as well, even better, than officers and men of the white divisions next to them. Their actions in the sector on both sides of the Moselle River proved it.

The sector was named after a town to the right of the Saint-Mihiel salient; the AEF took Saint-Mihiel on September 12–16, 1918, and the Marbache sector at this time was in French possession. Taking over the sector on October 9, the Ninety-second showed its mettle a month later, November 10–11. The mettle never gained much recognition, and if the commander of the new Second Army, Lieutenant General Bullard, would have had his way it would have received no notice at all. Bullard was a native of Georgia, the initial in his name—Robert L. Bullard—standing for "Lee." One of his favorite words in regard to the division was "niggah."[1] It is a point of interest that at this unlikely place and especially time, almost the end of the war, when the main body of U.S. troops, the American First Army, was sending shells into the four-track railroad at Sedan, First Army divisions crossing the Meuse along the great bend of the river between Sedan and Verdun, when Bullard's Second Army opened an attack to the east the only division that achieved anything was the Ninety-second.

## 1

The Marbache sector lacked attraction for several reasons. For one, geography alone made it impossible to be a *bon secteur*.[2] It was at the tail end of the long line held by the AEF, giving the impression that the American Army in France wished the African Americans out of sight if not out of mind. When the 368th Regiment encountered trouble in the Argonne—it was too much to say the regiment failed—the AEF dispersed the Ninety-second's 183rd Infantry Brigade to the divisions of the I Corps as labor troops, partly under supervision of the 317th Engineer Regiment. The prospect was that the other two U.S. corps in the Meuse-Argonne would absorb all the infantry regiments. For some reason General Pershing scotched that idea, that prospect, and on October 4 ordered the division to Marbache. Pershing, like his senior commanders, did not think black troops could fight. Marbache was quiet, and far away, and one might contend Marbache was a sort of military disposal.

The division arrived promptly and took over from the French Sixty-ninth Division. To the right of the sector were French troops, which created an awkward uncertainty. Being under their own corps command, part of the French Eighth Army, those troops were not subject to American orders; they might refuse, for their own reasons, to support the Ninety-second if the German enemy attacked. The French Army could fight when it wished, but after the Americans came in with hundreds of thousands of fresh troops they were almost evidently willing to let the new Associate, to use President Wilson's word (because the United States had no treaties of alliance with the British and French), do whatever fighting against the Germans that arose. Alsace-Lorraine, the portion of France in which the bulk of the U.S. Army was stationed, had been a longtime rest area for both German and French troops. The French, as did the Germans until aroused by the AEF in the Saint-Mihiel sector, preferred not to fight there, on the principle that if you did not attack the Germans, they would not attack you. French divisions to the east of the Ninety-second acted on this principle when fighting took place by the American Second Army on November 10–11, just before the Armistice. The Ninety-second was on its own.

If the French retreated in case of trouble, the division was in immediate danger, and for that reason an oversized company of 375 men of the 317th Engineers accompanied the division to Marbache. E Company, 317th, had the mission of being able at all times, men stationed nearby, to destroy bridges across the Moselle. In their spare time the company's engineers did frontline work with wire entanglements and trenches. The men were also slated to take part in a division attack scheduled for November 11, but the attack was called off not long after it started.[3]

The Marbache sector had the disadvantage of being the closest area of the American line to the German fortress of Metz. At the beginning of the formation of the AEF the fortress attracted American staff officers, and for months they planned an attack. The Saint-Mihiel salient was to be a passageway to Metz. Then the Allied commander in chief, Marshal Ferdinand Foch, asked Pershing, at the end of August 1918, to take the main body of AEF troops to the Meuse-Argonne, forty to fifty miles to the west, which meant halting the Saint-Mihiel attack once the Americans rolled up the salient. But Metz as a place of importance by no means disappeared, if only because American officers, planners and division commanders alike, kept Metz in mind as a goal, even while they had their hands full to the west. The Germans on their part, especially during the last two weeks of October, began to believe it might be possible to make Metz a hinge on which German troops along the fighting line to the west might swing back to a defensible line that would last through the winter of 1918–1919, at the end of which the German Army could recover from losses in such areas as the Meuse-Argonne. During the last two weeks of October, not long after the Ninety-second arrived in its new sector, the Americans under the new commander of the First Army, Gen. Hunter Liggett (Pershing retained his role as AEF commander in chief), stopped most attacks and obviously reorganized for a new general attack, which came on November 1–2. With this preparation and the attack itself, the importance of Metz to the German Army increased.

Metz was twenty miles from Pont-à-Mousson, to the north of which the Ninety-second disposed two of its regiments, the 365th and 366th. It was possible, and this had to be part of the calculation of General Ballou and his brigade and regimental commanders, that German garrisons in and around Metz might attack the African American division, perhaps thinking it more vulnerable than what few American divisions lay at the top of the old Saint-Mihiel salient. This, they might have calculated, would create a distraction from whatever attack General Liggett's First Army might be preparing.

The German Army in and close to Metz had an excellent position from which to attack. As the Germans retreated before attacks by the British, French, and Americans in the weeks and months after mid-July 1918, they sought to complete a long barrier to attackers; in some places, notably before Metz, it was five miles deep. Once the Ninety-second entered its sector it had to institute constant patrolling to be sure the enemy was not preparing, from the front of its strong line, to attack. The Americans could only hope that the French divisions to the right were similarly patrolling rather than preparing for a retreat in case of an attack.

The line the Ninety-second took over from the French Sixty-ninth was itself quite unattractive. Its front had the advantage of high ground, notably at the village of Norroy near which was a height known as Xon, at the top of a ridge that ran from the Moselle toward the east and eventually to ground occupied by the French Eighth Army.[4] The ridge at Xon was advantageous. The terrain in front was not, first because of a continuation of a swale that began at the Moselle and went east, narrowing but nonetheless discernible as it moved to the end of the Marbache sector. The swale was no-man's-land. Here the Ninety-second infantry had to patrol to be sure German troops had not infiltrated in force. The task, almost needless to say, was unending, for what looked harmless one day or night could not be so the next.

What made matters worse was that the Germans had created a salient that thrust down into the sector, behind which were obstacles to any attack from the American side. Like all salients, it doubled the line the Ninety-second had to patrol.

The defenses of the salient were essentially difficult to take. The principal difficulty was the Bois, or Forest, Fréhaut, a woods a mile square, in the salient's middle. At its base lay the Farm of Bel-air and to the other side a small woods by the name of Tête d'Or. If the Americans in an attack penetrated those two places, they came on the larger defenses of Fréhaut, sometimes occupied, others not. These were the usual, but usually effective, rows of heavy barbed wire, much of it new, and on east and west chevaux-de-frise reinforcements. At strategic places the enemy dug trenches for machine guns or riflemen, if necessary connecting the trenches. The machine gunners also had cement pillboxes. In the middle of Fréhaut the terrain declined to a valley, after which came an ascent.

Fréhaut had been impregnable. The commander of the Second Battalion, 365th Infantry, Ninety-second Division, Maj. Warner A. Ross, wrote that when the French attacked from the east they remained in the woods for about ten minutes. A second French attack was by Senegalese troops, no more successful. A third, by the Americans during Saint-Mihiel, like those of their predecessors, was repulsed. After the Ninety-second appeared, patrols frequently brought in bodies. When Ross led an attack on November 10, he was shocked to see gruesome remains hanging on the barbed wire. One of his men shook some wire, and a head fell off. Ross counted twenty-six American bodies or parts of bodies as his men went forward, in sad states of decomposure. He mulled over how no one, regardless of rank or station, if killed and hung on wire for two months, could look better than the individuals whose bodies he saw—"my own carcass or the carcasses of a king or even a queen, or of some wealthy notable, would look no better if it had been lying or hanging out in the weather."[5] At the base of Fréhaut and to its right a short distance lay the Bois de la Voivrotte, half the size of Fréhaut, which could protect any successful attack on Fréhaut.

Above Fréhaut lay La Côte, the highest hill in the vicinity. It was covered with trees up to the top. Here the Germans emplaced short-range artillery, judging from all the shell holes in the swale at the bottom. The trees at the top were covered by heavy guns from the defenses of Metz. Fréhaut was vulnerable to fire from La Côte and Metz even if the attackers' force was at first undetected. Attackers would need time to get through Fréhaut's wire defenses. La Côte had a tunnel up one side, by which observers could get to a tower and see everything down to Pont-à-Mousson, at the bottom of the positions of two of the Ninety-second's regiments.

La Côte had two protecting towns, Chambley on the left, Bouxieres on the right, both heavily garrisoned. In an analysis of the position of La Côte made by General Ballou just after the Armistice he pointed out that it was useless to try to take La Côte, after taking Fréhaut, unless the Ninety-second first took Chambley and Bouxieres.[6]

In addition to wire, machine guns with their trenches and pill-boxes, artillery light and heavy, the Ninety-second faced, as did the other divisions at the top of the Saint-Mihiel salient, major gas attacks. Here the African American troops did well compared to white divisions, which had spotty records. The Ninety-second was afflicted by all sorts of racial theorizing, engaged in by AEF officers. There was talk that black soldiers feared poison gas more than whites did, hence were more effective in preparing for it. This was nonsense; they were just better at the task. The theorists did not want to admit that, hence their theory. The leading historian of gas warfare in the divisions of the AEF, Rexmond C. Cochrane, who in the 1950s and 1960s prepared twenty studies, each of several dozen pages, under the aegis of the army's Chemical Warfare Service, wrote of the African Americans that they were almost the best among all divisions in following the advice of the CWS.[7] It would have been to the dismay of the gas theorists, had they known about it, that all of the division's gas officers were black, except for the DGO, division gas officer. Without exception they were efficient.[8] Their reports were timely and sensible.

Cochrane inquired from the records, as best he could, whether the standard mask, which it could be argued did not fit the faces of many African Americans, caused trouble, as gas officers feared. A new mask, bearing the name Tissot, solved that problem. At the end of the war it was just beginning to be distributed. The failure of the Ninety-second's gas records to record bad fitting for the standard mask seems to say that there were no serious mask problems.[9]

The only refusal to wear masks occurred with the commander of the 365th Regiment; Lt. Col. Answell E. Deitsch refused to take the advice of the regimental gas officer. It was the day before the Armistice, and the gas officer found Deitsch and the regimental staff (a major, two captains, and a lieutenant) carrying on without masks, this despite the concentration of mustard gas around regimental headquarters. Mustard demanded evacuation unless the most extreme consequences made unmasking mandatory. The regimental and later division gas officer warned Deitsch, who announced that his work required his and the staff's presence. He said he would not evacuate without brigade orders. This was 3:00

a.m., November 11. When ordered out by brigade orders, the entire staff had become casualties, together with 145 officers and men in the area who removed masks just after mustard shells came over.

Black gas officers were good at identifying or if not that then anticipating malingerers who wanted to get away from the front, "going along for the ride." As Cochrane wrote of these excellent gas officers, "None in the division was more aware than they of the excuse gas offered to get out of patrolling for a day or two or away from the battlefield, and their skepticism is recorded in their detailed gas attack reports."[10]

Of the several German gas attacks on the Ninety-second sector, the worst occurred early after the division's arrival, a calculated move by enemy gas units. Appearance of the Ninety-second's men together with those of the division west of them, the Seventh, both fresh divisions, persuaded gas units to move at once. The Germans had stocks of gas and for that reason were not hesitant to use them. Too, they had been the first to use gas on the western front in 1915. In following years they refined their use and were expert in dispensing just enough gas to keep their enemies nervous and even laboring under the disadvantage of handling frontline duties with masks on, which slowed their work. On the front of the American First Army the German foe used small if inconvenient amounts of gas until the Americans dumped tons in front of their line just before the Meuse-Argonne fourth attack on November 1–2. But east of the Meuse, from the initial entrance of American troops early in October, the German Army employed gas freely. Armee Abteilung C (Army Detachment C) ordered yellow cross, mustard, to forestall attacks. "Strong contamination shoots are important means of canceling the enemy's attack intentions or of destroying the enemy infantry in the process of preparation." A singular advantage of gas was that it was much more efficient, hence cheaper to use, than high-explosive shells. A calculation by Cochrane based on German use of gas on the Ninety-second showed that 320 HE shells produced one casualty, whereas ten gas shells did the same.[11]

In the months of September and October, more so in the latter month, the gas officers of the Ninety-second had their hands full in dealing with German gas. Counting the shells, one way of measuring their danger, was difficult. It required care to distinguish gas shells from ordinary shells. The enemy frequently mixed gas and heavy explosives in the same casing.

As mentioned, the first large German gassing occurred because of the appearance of the fresh division. The second came on Armistice Day in the misestimated belief that the German Army, driven out of the Meuse-Argonne, could still swing back on Metz.

The last factor that made Marbache a bad sector in addition to geography and gas was what happened on October 24–26, when the Ninety-second effectively lost from its command the 367th Infantry, which had to take station close to a regiment of the Seventh Division below the German-held village of Prény. This was against the desire of General Ballou. It was a bad move for the 367th, but Ballou could do nothing to prevent it. The shifting of the regiment removed it from whatever effect it could exert against the German foe. As for the regiment itself, the move wasted the time and energies of the 367th, a little matter of four thousand men placed in a corner and left there for the last three weeks of the war.

The movement of the 367th had something to do with the formation of the Second Army under General Bullard, announced on October 12, although the Second's staff had been forming for weeks. At the same time General Pershing promoted General Liggett as well as Bullard and put him in command of the First Army. Liggett did not take over until October 16 because Pershing had organized another attack by the First Army scheduled for October 14. The Second Army, it should be said, was a shadow of the First Army in size. By the time of the Armistice a total of twelve divisions passed through the Second Army, but when the Ninety-second virtually lost the 367th Regiment to the Seventh Division, the unit called the Second Army comprised only four divisions, its average size. At the west end of Bullard's thirty-mile line was the Thirty-third, tired from the Meuse-Argonne and service across the Meuse beginning October 8. It held the longest part of the line, twice as much as its sister divisions, followed by the Twenty-eighth, even more tired from the Meuse-Argonne, and then the Seventh, with no action at all, a raw division. Across the Moselle to the east was the Ninety-second.

The reason for sending the 367th Regiment has remained obscure. The only approximate explanation is that the Seventh, inexperienced, felt unsure of itself, and however it and the staff of the

Second Army felt about the qualities of the Ninety-second, it was more experienced than the Seventh. It is barely possible that General Bullard, with no respect for the African Americans, desired to make their position east of the Moselle even more awkward than it was by placing one of their four infantry regiments west of the Moselle. If Bullard and his staff were "out to get" the Ninety-second, it was a move of cleverness. The Second Army put the regiment almost out of touch with its already too far spread-out division. The 365th and 366th regiments were miles from Ballou's headquarters in the town of Marbache. The division's reserve regiment, the 368th, its reputation in tatters, even if wrongly, after its experience in the Argonne, was at the rear boundary of the sector, several miles below Pont-à-Mousson. From the top of the German salient including Fréhaut the two frontline regiments divided the area east of the Moselle. From Pont-à-Mousson to the village of Dieulouard on the river was seven miles. The village had the first bridge out of range of German artillery; all the bridges above were destroyed or subject to destruction. West of the Moselle lay the river's heights and then a large area, the Woevre plain. The plain was low and marshy in fall, winter, and spring, crossable only in summer.[12] It was in range of hostile artillery. By placing the 367th Regiment on the west side of such a barrier, any reinforcement of the Ninety-second was subject to delay while shuttled to Dieulouard and west to above Pont-à-Mousson. Observing this problem, Ballou proposed giving command of this regiment west of the Moselle to the commander of the Seventh. The Second Army refused to consider that possibility.[13]Distances in the Marbache sector were absurd any way one considered them. If they were a matter of command, it was seven miles from Pont-à-Mousson to Dieulouard, five more to Ballou's headquarters at Marbache, twenty more to Bullard at Toul—a good deal more from front to Bullard than to the even less friendly Metz.

## 2

The "reconnaissance in force," which the Second Army opened on the morning of November 10, in which the African American division showed its ability, far beyond that of the other three divisions then constituting General Bullard's command, was the result of a muddle. Such awkwardness is often the result of much planning and surely is nothing uncommon in American history. The AEF had produced many muddles, but by the time the Second Army undertook its reconnaissance the misestimates of the First Army had come almost to an end, the majority of divisions and their commanders acquiring considerable skill. The First Army was approaching the ability to act with machinelike efficiency, for the first time a match for the German enemy, matching also the best performance, which did not often occur, of the British and French armies.

Compared with the First Army, the Second Army was hardly a military organization, with little ability to do anything other than serve as a rest area.[14] General Bullard probably knew this, indeed could hardly avoid knowing it, since all he possessed was four divisions, two of them tired, the third without any experience, the other being the Ninety-second, the "niggahs." He hoped for many more divisions, perhaps transferred from the First Army as they crossed the Meuse toward his own forces. A few divisions were still coming over from the United States in October and November, and he might acquire them. His army, so-called, had scare value for the Germans, not something to misestimate; months earlier Pershing had established a mythical corps close to the Swiss border and sent the superannuated Maj. Gen. Omar Bundy to it, not telling Bundy the purpose of the charade, to bring German troops into the area and waste their fighting ability. Bullard was not in the best of health. He might have been a hypochondriac, for he kept a physician in attendance (although he was to live for many more years, dying in 1946). His biographer has written that he enjoyed being a lieutenant general and army commander, if in charge of a force unable to do much against the enemy; he had leisure, and reporters sought him out and wrote about Pershing's Second Army.

Bullard allowed his staff in Toul, led by Col. Stuart Heintzelman, the third generation of his family to serve with distinction in the U.S. Army, to enlarge the staff and plan actions for which he had insufficient troops. For this effort Heintzelman had the prospect of becoming a brigadier general, the rank that went with the office of an army chief of staff. It may have been the colonel who organized the Second Army, four divisions, with three corps: the XVII French Corps (Thirty-third U.S.), IV Corps (Twenty-eighth, Seventh), and, of all creations, VI Corps (Ninety-second, with General Ballou acting as commanding general). The three corps had chiefs of staff and in early November were acquiring officers and staffs.[15]

Whatever the pressures to build a shadow army with plans for attack, General Pershing himself began to manage the Second Army, of course through Bullard with the taking over of the First Army by Liggett, who was a powerful commander not to be managed. The commander in chief lacked activity, and when the First Army broke out toward the Meuse, Pershing elaborated the need for the Second Army to attack.[16] From what appears to have happened, Bullard felt he could not disagree, and was comforted by word that the tired Thirty-fifth Division, the Missouri-Kansas division defeated by the Germans in the first stage of the Meuse-Argonne, together with the new Eighty-eighth Division, was en route to his army. On November 2 Bullard alerted his divisions. There was planning for an attack on November 14, even though a German delegation was known to be going to see Marshal Foch and ask for terms of an armistice. The date of the Second Army's attack was changed to November 11. On the night of November 9, Pershing's headquarters telegraphed that the enemy was withdrawing everywhere and the Second Army was to develop the situation on its front. Bullard's corps and divisions reported their artillery and infantry were planning an attack but had not completed their plans. The Second Army ordered an advance anyway, for the enemy was pulling out. November 9, at 5:45 a.m., the Second Army issued field orders designating November 11 as D-day. At 6:30 p.m. it issued a field order initiating the order at once. The gas expert Cochrane found a scrawled pencil note on the field order sent to the Ninety-second: "This is some Field Order! No objective. Is it supposed to supplement No. 18 and No. 13? Suppositions! Great stuff!"[17]

With this lack of preparation it should have come as no surprise that the reconnaissance in force, or perhaps it was an attempted attack, failed miserably—save for the work of the despised Ninety-second Division. There remains, then, an account of what the African Americans did on the last two days of World War I. This was no effort to pull General Bullard's chestnuts out of the fire, for the Ninety-second, men and officers, showed the ability it had always possessed, if the division had been treated properly, which meant carefully, from the time it came into line after its supposed training in the Saint-Dié sector.

The Ninety-second's 367th Regiment went across the Moselle to below Prény, and was, as Ballou had sought to relate to the Second Army, difficult for him to command. Its task, unclearly set out as one might have expected, was to protect the Seventh Division's right flank when the Seventh's regiment, the 56th, attacked the town of Prény, which itself was to be a preliminary to an attack on the German-held town of Pagny a few miles to the north. The Germans were sensitive to any move that threatened Metz, even though Prény and Pagny were much farther from the fortress (which was to serve as a hinge) than the regiments of the African Americans east of the Moselle.

On the morning of November 10 the 56th Regiment of the Seventh duly attacked, going north to get into the east side of Prény where the terrain was easiest. A chateau lay on that side, and a seigneur of long ago may have put it there because he could send for his carriage and travel easiest into his town. As mentioned, the Seventh Division had no experience in line, and it badly miscalculated by attempting to attack Prény even from the east, perhaps drawing its inspiration from the seigneur's decision to place his chateau there. In days long past the owner of the chateau had only to call for his carriage. In 1918 the eastern approach was heavily wired; it was no thoroughfare. The regiment was caught in the wire.

The commander of the Seventh's Thirteenth Brigade, Brig. Gen. Alfred W. Bjornstad, heard from Col. A. L. Bump of the 56th and gave Bump authority to order the men to retire if he, the colonel, thought retreat advisable. Bump did, and the men came back with considerable casualties.

It was bad enough for the 56th to come back, but worse that the 367th had a difficult time finding the 56th, for the latter regiment had not moved toward Prény at the appointed Second Army attack time of 7:00 a.m. but chose its own time, 4:30. The early departure presumed either that the regiment believed it could get to Prény easier without the 367th or, by extending that logic, that the regiment of the Seventh or a higher commander within the division believed, before it started, it should take no assistance from a black regiment and have to share the accomplishment.

Gas expert Cochrane had one of his researchers check the Seventh's files, years later, and could find no evidence that the 56th left at 4:30. The files of the Ninety-second, regimental and other, are clear that the attack time for all units, in the field order from the Second Army, was 7:00.

After this fiasco the Second Army sent an inspector to General Ballou to ask why the 367th's men did not attempt to take Prény. The inspector told Ballou that to have tried this—mingling the 367th with the 56th caught in the wire—would have been suicidal. When after the war the Second Army drew up a balance sheet showing what the Ninety-second Division accomplished, it said that the African American division failed before Prény.

It is entirely possible that General Bjornstad was responsible for the wasting of the 367th Infantry Regiment of the Ninety-second Division, and the possibility should be set out. It might have been one of the turns of fortune that beset the African Americans—not their fault, but only a bad turn.

Alfred W. Bjornstad had been a rising figure in the U.S. Army and AEF, a man known for tactical brilliance. He entered the army at the time of the Spanish-American War, enlisted in the Minnesota National Guard, and after reaching the rank of captain during the Filipino Rebellion, his bravery noticed, remained in the service. Bullard had known him in the islands and upon becoming commanding general of the III Corps, organized soon after the I Corps, took him as his chief of staff. Bullard's corps was one of three that opened the Meuse-Argonne.

On the first day of the Meuse-Argonne, Bjornstad got into trouble. The Seventy-ninth Division in the III Corps's adjoining corps, the V, to the left, stalled before a height, Montfaucon, weakly held by the German foe. The question arose as to whether the adjoining Fourth Division, in the III Corps under Maj. Gen. John L. Hines, which had advanced rapidly, might send its unengaged 8th Brigade to the left, above Montfaucon, and snuff out the German defenders, a very tempting move and likely one of success. Hines inquired of his corps commander, Bullard, who was out, and the answer came from Bjornstad, who forbade the move as it would take a III Corps division into the adjoining corps area. It was a large opportunity missed; General Pershing afterward said the Seventy-ninth Division by stalling delayed the First Army's advance by a full day and gave the Germans enough time to bring in divisions and stop the First Army's initial attack—forcing the American Army into weeks of nearly futile frontal assaults. The commander of the 8th Brigade, Gen. E. E. Booth, spent more than twenty years after the war in obtaining a disavowal of the III Corps order by Bullard's errant chief of staff.

After this affair involving General Bjornstad there was a change of the III Corps commanders when Bullard went from the corps to the Second Army, with Hines receiving the corps command, and although no evidence has appeared that Hines believed he had a score to settle with Bjornstad, it is true that the corps' chief of staff, serving under Hines, lasted only ten days. When Bjornstad sent out an order without telling Hines, the latter admonished him, and on the second such order Hines went to army headquarters and presented a choice between himself and his chief of staff. Bullard in the Second Army picked up Bjornstad as commander of the 13th Brigade in the Seventh Division. Suffice to say that Bjornstad with this checkered background was capable, Bullard being his army commander, of changing an attack order that read 7:00 a.m. to 4:30 a.m.

No evidence has ever appeared that Bjornstad changed the attack order, but there is multitudinous testimony to the wartime general's arbitrary behavior. It came out during hearings in 1925 held by the Senate Military Affairs Committee over the proposal of the War Department to promote the former brigadier general, who after the war suffered a reduction in rank to colonel, his former rank. (During the war officers of the Regular Army could receive promotion in the National Army, the wartime army, and lost it upon disbandment of that force after the war.) A group of former officers of the 13th, including Colonel Bump, who had remained in the Regular Army, testified against his promotion.[18] They allowed as to how he had no talent for command. The hearings went to two volumes and included calling Generals Hines and Bullard. By this time Hines was army chief of staff, Bullard commander of a corps area, a peacetime command, centered on Governors Island in New York Harbor. Hines spoke against Bjornstad, Bullard less so but critical of what Bjornstad during the war told the French general Jean Degoutte; at that time Bullard commanded the First Division, and Degoutte was his army commander. Bullard on one occasion went from division headquarters to the front, with the express purpose of evacuating troops from an exposed village, Fismette, north of the Vesle River. Degoutte did not want Fismette evacuated, and when the French general happened to visit division headquarters Bjornstad told him what Bullard was about to do. Degoutte forbade it. Keeping the troops in Fismette caused dozens of American soldiers' deaths and capture by the Germans of several hundred men constituting Fismette's garrison.

Bjornstad's presence as brigadier of the 13th Brigade raised two possibilities for the 4:30 attack by his 56th Regiment. One was his habit of attempting to do everything by himself; he could not employ a staff properly but sought to handle everything on his own. General Hines saw this and believed it a major fault. Without presence of a staff to catch a chief of staff's errors and otherwise advise on the proper approach to problems, a single individual ran a risk of making and then compounding some error that had come to appear as the right and proper course—such as, say, a belief that a 4:30 attack time was what the Second Army field order allowed if it did not so prescribe.

Another of Bjornstad's errors lay similarly in the belief he could do tasks better than his staff, behind which was his sense that he was more intelligent than his assistants or for that matter superiors. He prided himself on his military knowledge. In actual fact his memory was unreliable; during the hearings he turned an important question completely around. The question arose over his refusal on September 26 to allow the Fourth Division to enter the area of the V Corps. According to his memory General Bullard had remained in the III Corps headquarters, Bjornstad had gone into the field, and Bullard had refused permission to the Fourth Division.[19] East of the Moselle, when the reconnaissance in force began at 7:00, what happened was far more clear, and it was all to the credit of officers and men of the two regiments of the Ninety-second Division on the line.

Little need be said about the attacks against two woods, the Bois de la Voivrotte, which was to the right of the much larger Bois

Fréhaut, or of the tiny Bois de Cheminot, which lay in the direction
of Metz and would have had importance if the Metz attack should
have followed. Voivrotte took attention of three companies of a battalion of the 366th Regiment, Cheminot two platoons. The attack
on Voivrotte, supervised by General Ballou, who went up from
Marbache to watch and if necessary intervene, was in two phases.
The first, by the battalion of Maj. Alfred E. Sawkins, moved up to
the top of the woods and met a fury of machine guns and shells
from guns on La Côte and batteries surrounding Metz, together
with heavy shelling by the enemy's gas detachments, and Sawkins
took his men back to the southern edge, to the displeasure of Ballou.
The result was a second attack: Ballou said the men could escape
the gas, their principal problem, by moving above the woods rather
than seeking areas where the gas would have no opportunity to
blow away. Sawkins started a new attack at 3:00 a.m., November
11, and retook the woods. For Sawkins it was understandable that
he could easily hesitate to lead his men, and at 3:00 in the morning
the major did it. The investigator of African American behavior,
Charles Williams, remarked that the men of Sawkins's battalion in
the 366th would follow him. "Of Major Sawkins it is said that whatever fare his officers had he shared with them, that he worked for
the interest of both officers and men at all times, and that the spirit
of his men when he went into battle was always high."[20]

East of the Moselle the main action by far was the move into
Bois Fréhaut by the Second Battalion of the 365th under Major
Ross. A natural soldier like Sawkins, he had a battalion reinforced
by machine guns, 37mm guns, Stokes mortars, a total of 1,250 men.
Ross had taken over the battalion on October 4. All captains and
lieutenants were African Americans. He knew he had to work with
what he had. Too, it was such a difference, his respect for his officers and men, in comparison with the aloofness of white officers of
the 368th in the Argonne.

When orders came down on November 9 that the reconnaissance
would take place not November 14, nor eleventh, but November
10, the major decided on the move that ensured the success of his
battalion: at 7:00 p.m. on November 9 he assembled all officers, and
from then until 3:00 a.m. he went over what they would do and how
he wished them and their men to do it in Fréhaut. He overlooked

nothing. Each officer received a map with directions and after study showed Ross exact knowledge of his assignment. "I attribute the battalion success," Ross wrote in his after-action report, "largely to this conference which lasted 8 hours."[21] His book about his battalion, published by himself in 1920, is filled with religious observations, and it was in part an address made to his former officers and men in Chicago. Historians and military writers have chosen to ignore it. Ross in civil life was a lawyer who spent his later years in Lafayette, Indiana; he had no military background prior to the war. But there is much to learn from the book. It is the story of an intelligent man who found himself with what some of his fellow officers failed to see, a leadership problem, and he solved it.

Major Ross expected his battalion's attack on Bois Fréhaut to change the Ninety-second's reputation, and sadly such was not to take place: "The generals commanding our Division and brigade seemed very anxious that this operation prove a success. Up to this time the Division had not accomplished anything very startling in the way of capturing German strongholds, but here, before the expected armistice went into effect, was an opportunity to prove the Division's ability and worth and refute any whisperings that might be in the air. In other words, to quote one of the high ranking superiors, full and real success here would forever give the division a leg to stand on."[22]

It is entirely possible that the reason after the war and publication of his book Ross seldom spoke of his wartime exploit with the Second Battalion at Fréhaut was the failure of the Ninety-second to profit from it. Ross's son, seventeen years old when the major died in 1940, says his father told him nothing about what happened. Ross kept no papers; there was nothing other than his book and what papers remained with division records.

Of his leadership there could be no question. The book relates that he brought up none of his officers to efficiency boards, the course taken by the 368th Regiment's infantry majors (see below, pages 100ff). He tried two men by summary court and acquitted both.

The attack from the outset was well managed.[23] Ross credited his brigade commander, General Barnum, with allowing the battalion to proceed, as quickly as possible, above Bel-air Farm rather than cross the mile of no-man's-land below the farm and wait for artillery support. He took the companies through the farm, cutting wire as quickly as the men could; using large cutters on the heavy wire, men following bending back cut edges to help others get through. All this haste was well conceived, for German guns soon ranged in on the farm, gunners reckoning the battalion's presence because of the Ninety-second's barrage coming in, as it needed to, above Bel-air. For Ross and men this initial move accompanied by two fires, their own and that of the enemy, was trying, for they occupied an area barely large enough to protect them. German artillerists began to walk their barrage north, and there was need to grit teeth, in hope the fire was not close enough. Fortunately, casualties were not numerous. When Captain Green with H Company moved to the east to garrison the edge of Fréhaut against German troops coming in from the defenses of Metz, it was a sign that the attack was going as planned.

A wise move by Ross was to put his post of command in an easily described place to which runners, the battalion's only means of communication, could find their way. He placed the PC in the southern end of the Bois de la Tête d'Or. As the day wore on, fog lifting, the hole from which Ross and staff worked showed its disadvantage, its visibility, and a German plane found it. According to the major the enemy fired thirty-five shells into the PC, and the thirty-sixth caved in the hole. Shrapnel rained, but the major remained after digging the hole out. The plane had gone away, in belief that thirty-six shells erased everything. To change the PC would have disrupted the network of runners. When Green's company was attacked, as expected, Green needed reinforcements, and the runner appeared in barely enough time to get more machine guns to the company. The PC was gassed, as its occupants believed would happen, and they wore sag paste for what protection it offered, and after the gassing scattered chloride of lime. The gas did little more than cloud their vision, was not strong enough to force a move.

Fréhaut in some ways resembled the Argonne. There were ravines, notably the large ravine across the middle of the woods. There were steep hills and patches of heavy undergrowth. All this was added to by the preparations to the German defensive position improved over a four-year period. Wire was everywhere, together with traps and mines, reinforced by dugouts and a complete system of telephone and signal lines. In such an obstacle course the woods made everything worse by shielding attacking units, creating the same situation that dogged battalions of the 368th—men disappeared after advancing a few feet. The difference was that with the eight-hour drill before the battalion's jump-off, each unit had instructions, knew where it was going, trusted its white commander far more than those in the Argonne.

By 9:35 a.m. all platoons assigned to the first line but two were on their objectives. The runners brought in word of each unit's arrival. Machine-gun nests delayed the two units, but they came up. By 10:00 liaison had been established between units, and everyone was digging in. Men were emplacing machine guns and mortars as German tactics always favored counterattacks, and in the Ninety-second's sector that also meant gas. Ross wrote a message, put into the aluminum shell on the leg of a pigeon, watched the bird rise and circle, turn and head south fifteen miles to Marbache. The message was that the Second Battalion had reached all objectives, was holding, and would continue to hold.

The major afterward, after the Armistice, sent in his casualty list: one officer severely gassed, four gassed; nine men killed, twenty wounded, ten missing.

**FIVE**

# Conclusion

THE REPUTATION OF THE Ninety-second Division was not high before its 368th Regiment went into the Argonne Forest for five days. Thereafter it settled into the basement of divisional reputations. The reason was twofold. For one thing, the white officers of the division who in the Ninety-second were for the most part senior officers, field grade officers to employ the army phrase for grades of major and above, believed that blacks could not make good officers of any sort, nor could their men fight. The reason was a racial difference: the black race was mentally inferior. The other part of the reason for the low appraisal of African Americans as fighting men was a series of events that afflicted the Ninety-second after the end of the war. Those events had their beginnings in the Marbache sector where Generals Ballou and Bullard could not get along. The appearance of their antagonism was all in favor of Bullard, who was a canny maneuverer against the rough edges of Ballou's personality. History, by which one means what Americans in subsequent years thought of the Ninety-second, came down against the division.

Because of racism and events that followed the Argonne, the Ninety-second's achievements were lost from view. In the Argonne and despite the retreat of the Second Battalion and the collapse of the Third, the First Battalion managed to move forward to Binarville, with a few men going beyond. If one considered this performance against the achievements of white divisions during the first attack of the First Army in the Meuse-Argonne, the showing of the 368th Regiment was not so bad. In the I Corps to the right the three divisions did not do well, with the Seventy-seventh moving ahead in its part of the Argonne with a slowness that was contrary to what General Pershing asked of his divisions. The second division of the corps, the Twenty-eighth, did likewise. The third, the Thirty-fifth, collapsed in the field, gave up territory it had taken, and had to be relieved and sent to a portion of the line where there was little action and it could refit and recover its nearly lost morale. In the next corps, the V Corps, the performances of all three of the divisions were so poor that General Pershing withdrew all three; the third of the V Corps divisions, the Seventy-ninth, did so badly that it held up the advance of all the divisions of the First Army for an entire day while the division fumbled in front of Montfaucon, where two of its regiments stalled before a minuscule German force. The last of the corps in line, the III Corps, did fairly well but not spectacularly, by any means. In the second and third attacks of the First Army, over the next weeks, the Americans managed only to inch their way forward against the defending German divisions.

A little trouble with a single regiment of the Ninety-second Division was not worth the attention it received. Meanwhile, the achievements of the division's engineer regiment and its artillery brigade, both units successful by any measure—those successes were ignored. The account of the 317th Engineers, written with admiration by Lieutenant Colonel Cassidy, together with two volumes of photographs, went into the division's files, and the present writer believes he was the first person to look at Cassidy's history and the photographs after the passage of nearly a century since the achievements they celebrated. The quick training and excellent firing of the 167th Field Artillery Brigade were praised by General Sherburne, whose blunt statements of what happened were notable; they lay buried in the files of the U.S. Army Military History Institute, a part of the Army War College in Carlisle Barracks, Pennsylvania.

The same can be said for the work of the Ninety-second's three infantry regiments on line during the Second Army's attack on November 10–11, 1918, all of which did well, the Second Battalion of the 365th Regiment making the only notable advance of any unit in General Bullard's army, the other regiments succeeding at their assignments, all this when the three white divisions of the army failed to do anything.

1

The U.S. Army's appraisal of the usefulness of African Americans in the military was a rude proposition, as befitted a subject on which Regular Army officers had thought little for a long time. During the Civil War both sides used black troops; the South only after the war turned against Southern forces, and the region's great need became soldiers, of any ability or racial background. To the North the enlistment of blacks seemed ill-advised, if logical to abolitionists, and the North accepted their enlistment or draft almost as reluctantly as did the South—there was willingness to accept blacks as cannon fodder, as in the episode of the Crater in Virginia in 1864. After the War of the Rebellion the army enlisted black troops for service primarily in the West, which area for thirty years occupied the small postwar army's 25,000 men and officers, not even the table-of-organization size of a World War I U.S. division. The army in the West after the war saw difficult, even arduous, action, in which the black regiments did well, probably as well as the whites. In the Spanish-American War the buffalo soldiers did very well, heroic, at San Juan Heights, fighting with white units such as the 71st New York and the 1st Volunteer Cavalry (Theodore Roosevelt's Rough Riders). But during all the years after 1865 the army was no intellectual place, its officers in the East centered in small "forts" in or near cities dreaming of the fast-receding Civil War, officers in the West spending time in similar reminiscences or in drinking on post. After the Spanish-American War there was a little time for meditating on the place of black troops in the army, and more officers to meditate, for the army increased to the size of 130,000 in 1917 when the war in Europe brought in the Americans: by that time the army's ideas on inclusion of African Americans, what such troops could do and what they could not, had solidified. During World War I the thinking of officers of the army lay largely against inclusion of blacks in the AEF, a different war from the American West and the Spanish of 1898 and subsequent actions in the Philippines, Central America, the Caribbean, and Mexico. It is safe to say, indeed this is what happened, that organization of the Ninety-second Division (the Ninety-third was only a matter of four infantry regiments, no supporting troops) was a political rather than military measure. It was necessary because of the nascent civil rights movement, evident in northern cities where black voters had taken on importance. The movement was not large enough to require major efforts, and organization of the Ninety-second was no major operation. The philosophy behind it was preventive. The zeal with which the War Department's officers promoted the division was doubtful. There nonetheless was an effort, backed by Secretary Baker, if not by President Wilson whose lack of zeal for African Americans was fairly well known; Wilson in his first term, beginning in 1913, allowed segregation of the government's civil departments in the nation's capital. The army, organizing the Ninety-second, did its nominal best, and some officers such as the then Colonel Ballou came into the organizing who were genuinely favorable to black rights. Others, such as the engineer officers Cassidy and Earl Brown, discovered their men were as competent, if directed properly, as whites; General Sherburne to his delight found his artillery brigade as good as it could be. Ballou's chief of staff in the Ninety-second, Colonel Greer, took assignments because of the opportunity for promotion and perhaps opportunity to move out of the division to more attractive assignments. Military writer Millett espied a good deal of careerism among white officers of the Ninety-second.[1]

The roots of the U.S. Army's thinking about blacks, then, were not deep and not far removed from ideas about black Americans in general, in North or South—the Middle West and West, accustomed to fewer blacks, had opinions of a superficial sort but less fixed. The young Harry S. Truman in rural Missouri near the farm town of Independence wrote ignorantly of visits to the black ghetto of Kansas City, employing words his detractors years later seized upon and elevated to far more importance than the remarks deserved. When early in his presidency he discovered the truth, he turned his opinions 180 degrees.

In appraising the army's attitude during World War I, the best resort, because the opinions are detailed and came from an army officer of experience with African American troops, is the remarks of Major General Hay, the same who commanded the 184th Brigade of the Ninety-second comprising the 367th and 368th regiments. Hay served more than twenty years with the 24th

Cavalry. He commanded the 184th Brigade of the Ninety-second until October 25, 1918, when promotion to major general sent him out of the division. Unlike his fellow infantry brigadier in the Ninety-second, General Barnum, he wrote easily, expressed himself well, and when after the war Colonel Greer asked privately for his opinion offered it in more particulars than one might have thought possible.[2]

"Because of inherent weaknesses in negro character," General Hay related, black Americans required a much longer time than whites to learn anything. The point was important, but suffices to fasten on the word *inherent*, which says he did not see any possibility of improvement. His primary point was that African Americans differed mentally from whites.

Hay's ideas were similar to those of many, indeed most, of his army contemporaries, and after stating this primary point about inferior mental capacity he offered almost a cascade of opinions that were not corollaries of his idea about mental weakness but came from experience, he said, with black troops. One of the general's ideas was that blacks suffered from a lack of initiative. He took it as a "given" property of the black race. Because of lack of initiative black soldiers required longer to learn anything. The usual estimate of the time lag between African American and white learning was that blacks took twice the white requirement. Hay said that the African American officer showed the same incapacities. "The fact that he holds a commission leaves him still a negro." Black officers were a dismal failure in training, administration, and combat. Because of the black mind, it stood to reason that black officers could not lead. This was a crucial failure. That officer was a failure in battalion staff posts, in platoons and companies. Such failing accounted for failure of all the white divisions, Hay knew, so it necessarily was crucial, indeed had been so proved.

The general recalled other black delinquencies. The black leaders he knew were too concerned with their appearances, spent time on that trivial pursuit. African American officers were too much concerned about having a good time.

If officered by blacks, African American troops had to be used only as pioneer or labor troops. Even then their usefulness was questionable.

When used with white officers, black troops could manage some tasks. General Hay, unlike many of his fellow officers, believed they could make excellent—he used the word—soldiers. Under white leaders they showed utmost bravery, without fear of personal consequences. The French Army, American officers learned, used black troops such as the Senegalese "black demons" as shock troops. Beyond the possibility of fine fighters—under white leaders—Hay did not go.

White leaders were essential, for Hay made a comment that typified the beliefs or experiences of the majority of American officers: blacks would not follow black officers. He saw very few black officers with African American troops, none among the four peacetime Regular regiments. He nonetheless declared there would be no following. This was a condition, not a theory. The general said he had seen this time after time.

He concluded his remarks about blacks in the military by offering his opinion on racial equality. The question, he wrote, was not open to discussion. "I am unalterably opposed to mixing of Negro and white officers, under any circumstances, other than those which arise in the performance of military duties." Black officers, the general posited, were more concerned about trying to force racial equality than learning their military duties.

In his letter to Colonel Greer in which he listed the above conclusions, he asked the colonel to keep them confidential. When he commanded the 184th Brigade, which included the 368th Regiment when it was in the Argonne, he did his best, and while the results did not surprise him, he was bitterly disappointed.

Brig. Gen. W. P. Jackson, like Hay, had experience with African American troops and was with the Ninety-second Division as colonel of the 368th before his promotion.[3] He served nine years with the 24th Infantry, eight months commanding the 368th. By and large Jackson agreed with General Hay. His approach to black troops was to treat them like grownup children. He had been unsure of the 368th's captains, who had been noncoms in the black Regular regiments. "I did not have a captain," he wrote, "who possessed sufficient executive ability to direct his five subordinates and to command a company of 250 men." He wrote Greer after the war that he thought African Americans capable of being captains.

He sensed, however, that the times were against black leadership. Interestingly, he blamed the trouble of obtaining captains with leadership qualities on the way in which African American children grew up, not inherent lack of mental ability. Youngsters did not obtain moral training at home, not the morality that white boys obtained. In his opinion, "the tendency of the colored boy of the present day is to become more worthless, considered as a class, than was the case twenty-five or thirty years ago." The tendency toward shiftlessness was so marked that, he concluded, the army should not commission black Americans.

A pronounced exponent of the inadequacy of African Americans for military service in all branches and certainly as officers in company grades, not to mention ranks above captain, was Col. George H. McMaster, assistant inspector of the First Army during 1917–1918, who spent twelve years with the 24th Infantry.[4] McMaster was important because he was a trenchant writer and did not mind expressing his opinions. His assignment to the inspector general's office in the First Army sharpened his willingness to pass judgment. He had left the 24th Infantry in 1907 and that year sent in a report on the use of blacks in the Regular Army. In 1913, along with James A. Moss, who became colonel of one of the infantry regiments in the Ninety-second, and the then colonel R. L. Bullard, he submitted another memorandum concerning use of black troops and black officers. After the Armistice McMaster volunteered to take command of the 365th Infantry of the Ninety-second Division, for the purpose of taking it home and supervising its disbandment, serving an eventful two months during which, faced with what he considered disruptive activity by black officers of his regiment and of officers of the Ninety-third Division, he preferred charges against 112 officers. While aboard the liner *Olympic* (sister ship to the *Titanic*), they signed a round-robin to the ship's army commander, a general, asking that seating in the fore and aft dining rooms be assigned according to rank rather than whites to the first-class dining room, blacks if not second-class then the aft dining room, distinctly less prestigious than the grand saloon.

McMaster could not have been beloved by his charges. In his inimitable way he set out his knowledge. "No one but a Colonel who has commanded one of these Regiments, with mixed officers, knows the tact and common sense needed to keep down friction; and no one knows better than he, the amount of work required of the selected white staff officers and the latter's mistrust of the ability of the colored company commanders to get things right."

Colonel Greer, the Ninety-second's chief of staff, equal in rank to Colonel McMaster, was equally specific in backing up everything McMaster said.[5] After the war he gave his views, like McMaster, from bitter experience, he wrote, from thirteen months in the Ninety-second. He was not a West Pointer but a Regular, and held a bachelor's degree from the University of Tennessee and a law degree from the University of Minnesota.

Greer knew extraordinary details about blacks in the military. Only 15 percent, no more than 20 percent, of drafted African Americans were capable of being soldiers, and otherwise might do well as teamsters and chauffeurs. When in training he advised close order drill, as blacks admired ceremonies and were quick to learn drill. Blacks could not stand in heavy combat; they would sneak to the rear. They lacked patriotism and thought they were in the service not to fight but to advance their race. It was a well-known fact, familiar to all people who knew blacks, that the average black was cowardly. The medical department of the army had found out from twenty thousand cases that only one-tenth of 1 percent had the mental qualifications to become officers. Colonel Greer said he had observed black officers carefully and that "taken as an average their ignorance was colossal."

In the above analysis a single topic remains the belief of many white officers that blacks harbored a physical hunger for white women. It was a subject of talk, undoubtedly encouraged by the lack of racial feeling in France. It was encouraged by the absence of white Americans from their country, their loneliness and need for topics of conversation in the midst of the dullness and boredom of so much of military existence. There also was the proclivity of people, of any group, to talk about subjects on which they knew virtually nothing.

For the commanding officers in the Ninety-second mentioned above, one finds no speculation on this subject, and the presumption must be that they were too busy to fasten their minds on it. In two instances officers of rank did speculate, and their comments need mention in detail, if only because the commentaries were typical of the era in which they made them.

Colonel McMaster, who believed himself competent to explain the black issue in the army, was fixated on the African American desire for rape.[6] Blacks were sexual brutes, he wrote. Ever the theorist, a military logician, with ideas he would have described as reasoning, in his letter to Greer he opened this special subject with a truism: "The question of rape of white women is a disagreeable one." He followed with another, that it must be approached with the desire to ascertain the facts. He followed with a fact that, in regard to the numbers of men he supervised while commanding the 365th after the war, approximately four thousand, in the month the regiment was in France under his command, January 16 to February 16, 1919, he encountered three cases of attempted rape. While at Brest just before embarkation it was necessary for him to turn over to the authorities one black officer who made indecent remarks to a white nurse. (The nurse may have misstated them, perhaps imagined them, but this possibility did not enter the colonel's calculus.) McMaster did not relate what happened to all these four men out of four thousand cases, simply remarked them. He followed by telling Greer that he had seen an order forbidding black soldiers to have any relations with white women. Such an order could hardly have been issued "without grave justification therefore."[7] This order must have been the one issued when the Ninety-second was in Saint-Dié after the shooting of the French nurse, in which the commander of the 184th Brigade, General Hay, fastened almost immediately upon a man in one of his regiments, who had been drunk and whose whereabouts and purposes were unclear.

The surprising analysis of the rape question was not Colonel McMaster's but the statements by the Ninety-second's chief of staff, Colonel Greer, in a letter of December 6, 1918, to Senator Kenneth D. McKellar of Tennessee. Greer was a writer of precision and facility, like McMaster; not loyal to General Ballou, he viewed the usefulness of black Americans in the military, certainly the usefulness of black officers, in the same way as the other commanding officers of the division. But what was surprising was his animus against African Americans on the rape question. One might well ask how he could have said such things. On this point he provided no answers, only statements. Speaking of the men and officers over whom the colonel exercised command he opined: "They have in fact been dangerous to no one except themselves and women." The colonel blamed black misconduct of this sort entirely on black officers. In regiments of engineers and artillery where supervised by white officers there had been only a single case of rape. "The undoubted truth is that the colored officers neither control nor care to control the men. They themselves have been engaged largely in the pursuit of French women, it being their first opportunity to meet white women who did not treat them as servants."The successor of Booker T. Washington at Tuskegee Institute in Alabama, the distinguished Robert R. Moton, went to France at the behest of Secretary of War Baker to investigate the circumstances of service of black Americans in the Ninety-second and the separate regiments of the Ninety-third Division, together with the conditions provided for pioneer companies and those of labor companies, including stevedore companies. Moton did this at risk of criticism from civil rights groups that believed he would be acting as an Uncle Tom, groups that attributed such behavior to Washington himself. Moton saw a larger need for his oversight and ignored the criticism. Hearing the stories of misbehavior in the Ninety-second, he asked Maj. Gen. Charles H. Martin, who succeeded General Ballou in command of the Ninety-second, what was the state of affairs. Martin said there were twenty-seven rape cases. Moton asked for the papers. He obtained seven files, and of those cases two men were convicted. AEF general headquarters reversed one of these convictions.[8]

Maj. A. E. Patterson, judge advocate of the Ninety-second after the war, informed Charles Williams of the figures for rape in the division: "Ten soldiers were tried for assault with intent to rape. Five of those were bona fide efforts to accomplish that crime. The other five were simple assaults with no evidence to support the charge of assault with intent to commit rape. Three of the cases were actual rape cases, only one of which was in the 92nd Division."[9]

In conclusion about the outlook of white commanders in the Ninety-second in regard to African American troops and the African American company-grade officers throughout the infantry regiments, according to Williams, black officers found it nearly impossible to cooperate with commanding officers. They were never taken into the confidence of the whites. The latter "rarely ever" questioned them about matters affecting the men.[10] Here the commander of the Second Battalion, 368th Regiment, the unit that first went into the Argonne, on September 26, Major Elser, put his finger on the problem. Of the three battalion commanders and the colonel of the regiment, only Elser appears to have thought out, in any serious way, the racial situation of the 368th. When his men got into trouble during the first two nights in the line and each time, with the exception of one or two companies, came back to the trench from which they advanced, Elser broke into tears, comforted and for a time harbored, sent back to rest, by the regiment's colonel. Elser was the only battalion officer of the regiment who was a Regular and was promoted after the action. In his long interrogation after the war by Colonel Rivers he was not the best testifier, tended to wander and be imprecise. But he was clear on the racial issue. White officers, he said, were constantly on the defensive toward not only black troops but also African American officers "in their attitude on the matter of race prejudice." The Ninety-second was filled with this tension. "White officers were constantly defending." Both sides, he said, were urging a conservative attitude on any race question in all situations. This effort by the white officers was never relaxed "for one minute." It was, he told Rivers, a very difficult problem for even those of long experience in such matters.[11]

## 2

In the final weeks of the war, when the Ninety-second Division was in the Marbache sector, and in the days just after the Armistice, a series of events took place that, together with the racism that dogged the division from its beginning, ensured the division's lack of reputation. One trouble followed another. Some of the difficulty was an undoubted rivalry between General Ballou and General Bullard: to each other they were oil and water. Whatever the reasons for the mess that resulted, no one seemed able to stop the confusions; it was not possible for lower or higher officers of the AEF, in or out of the division, to call a halt, out of common sense.

The initial action in the series was by Major Norris of the Third Battalion of the 368th Regiment. Norris, being a New York lawyer, and without any regard for the delicacy of race relations with his battalion, regiment, or division, put up eleven of his company-grade officers to go before efficiency boards, which had the power to divest officers of their commissions. Major Elser of the Second Battalion, whose companies could not stay on the line in the Argonne and each night drifted back to their starting places, put up fourteen. Major Merrill, the soldier of fortune who advanced his companies by pistol point, gave the names of six officers. This made a total of thirty names of officers of the 368th whose commissions were in danger (the figures come from testimony by the regimental commander, Colonel Brown, whose estimates within the battalions added to thirty-one).

If matters had stopped with men going before the boards, that would have been bad enough, for taking away commissions was in itself a drastic step. It would embarrass any officer so moved against. But the division's judge advocate, Lieutenant Colonel Packer, threw this entire issue into the open by taking the first five names in the list given him by Norris and putting those individuals up for court-martial. Four were from Company I, two first lieutenants, two second lieutenants. One name, a captain, was from Company K.

General Ballou should have talked to his judge advocate, sternly, and informed him that he, the division commander, forbade such action. If Ballou had known his division lawyer, he might have told him the reason, which was the delicacy of such a move, coming on the preceding delicacy of what Norris and the other majors, apparently encouraged by Brown, had done. Instead, Ballou joined his other white officers, in his flighty way, by adding to the conflagration with a memorandum of October 12, in which he listed all the officers up for boards, the specific incapacities of each, asked removal of the officers from his division, and sent the memorandum to the IV Corps, the then supervisory command for the Ninety-second Division.

Ballou's comments about each officer were scathing.[12] They had to be grossly overdrawn:

| | |
|---|---|
| 2nd Lt. Benjamin Bettis | worthless |
| Capt. Elija Reynolds | inefficient and worthless |
| 2nd Lt. Edw. Robertson | general inefficiency and cowardice |
| 2nd Lt. Chas. B. Robinson | unfitted to be an officer |
| 1st Lt. Merriam C. Hayson | general inefficiency |
| 1st Lt. Harold Quivers | general inefficiency |
| Capt. Richard Simmons | general inefficiency |
| 1st Lt. Levi Alexander | physically unfit |
| 1st Lt. Francis M. Dent | untrustworthy and generally worthless |
| 1st Lt. Azzie B. Koger | failed to command platoon in action |
| 1st Lt. Douglas J. Henderson | had been before board, no action yet rec'd |
| 2nd Lt. Frank C. Clark | went to hospital morning of battle |
| 2nd Lt. Wm. T. Grady | fled or withdrew without orders |
| 1st Lt. P. W. Jones | fled or withdrew without orders |
| 2nd Lt. C. W. Marshall | fled or withdrew without orders |
| Captain Bob Thomas | failed to lead his company into actions as ordered |
| Captain C. A. Sandridge | allowed company to disintegrate and flee |
| 1st Lt. James Lomack | fled or withdrew with platoon without orders |
| 2nd Lt. Fritz Alexander | failed to halt or control his men |
| 2nd Lt. H. W. Johnston | fled or withdrew with platoon without orders |
| 2nd Lt. Jefferson Meeks | failed to halt or control his men and fled with them |
| 1st Lt. Judge Cross | ) |
| 1st Lt. H. R. Crawford | ) |
| 2nd Lt. R. W. Cheers | ) |
| 2nd Lt. R. M. Johnston | ) |
| Captain Daniel Smith | ) Led their men in a cowardly and inexcusable retreat. This occurred twice. |
| 1st Lt. L. G. Koger | ) |
| 1st Lt. W. T. Webb | ) |
| 2nd Lt. W. W. Scott | ) |
| 2nd Lt. Andrew Reed | ) |

The error of the above listing and sending it to the IV Corps stands readily to mind. It showed little or no understanding of a fundamental aspect of administration, namely, the unwisdom of sending anything out of one's own organization that can be settled inside. Ballou, as mentioned, should have taken the efficiency board and especially court-martial issues in hand and squelched them and by no means showed what might be interpreted as his own lack of judgment in allowing incompetent—if they were—officers to handle men on a front line, in these cases the Argonne.

Then there was another perhaps not unsurprising lack of sensitivity on the part of the basically attractive, because he was the friend of his African American men and officers, commanding general of the Ninety-second. Ballou appears to have known little, probably nothing, of what was to happen on the very day, October 12, he sent his memorandum to the IV Corps. This was the elevation of Major General Bullard of, at that time, the III Corps to command the Second Army. As a Regular colonel before the war Ballou must have known Bullard's southern prejudices, Bullard's dislike of "niggahs."

Bullard, taking control immediately, gave the impression of stopping the moves in course at the Ninety-second, but did nothing of the sort. Barely installing himself in his new post, he had plenty of duties to keep him busy. His three divisions, plus the Ninety-second, were all in need of attention. The white divisions were in need of counsel, for the Thirty-third and Twenty-eighth were worn out from being in line in the Meuse-Argonne, the Seventh Division a force with no battle experience. The Seventh, closest to the German garrisons outside of Metz, was not even putting out patrols to see what it might face if the Germans attacked. Instead of dealing with these division weaknesses, Bullard went up from Toul to the 368th Regiment, in reserve for the Ninety-second, and spent three or four days inquiring at random of men and officers about their experiences in the Argonne, seeking, so he said, to discover the nature of that problem. He then, contrary to what he should have done, allowed the courts-martial to go ahead.

Meanwhile, Ballou made a move that Greer should have prevented if possible, and this was to send a proposal to each of the thirty officers on his list giving them an opportunity to redress their records by volunteering to lead patrols. "General Ballou was a great

believer in the colored man, and his ability as a leader," Colonel
Brown told Colonel Rivers, "and wanted to give them a last chance,
these officers who had been recommended for an efficiency board."[13]
One or two may have taken up the proposal but no more than that,
for to have done so would have admitted guilt, which none of them
did. Major Elser did not know what happened to his recommended
officers. He considered the issue between Ballou and the officers.
Replies of the latter came first to his attention for transmission to
division headquarters. They were in sealed envelopes, and Elser felt
he should not unseal and read them.[14]

The courts-martial followed, in the last days of October and early
in November. Of Norris's first five officers three of the lieutenants—
Cross, Crawford, and Cheers—and Capt. Daniel Smith were convicted
under the Seventy-fifth Article of War that they did "shamefully retreat
and run away from the enemy." They were to be "shot to death with
musketry." 2d Lt. Robert M. Johnston was to be "dismissed from the
service and to be confined at hard labor at such place as the reviewing
authority may direct for the term of his natural life." General Bullard
sought suspension of the sentences and the officers dismissed. He
tried for suspension by the judge advocate of GHQ by invoking technicalities, but that officer would not go along.[15] The sentences of death,
the judge advocate and Bullard knew, would not have confirmation
by President Wilson, who routinely denied all such requests by the
army. This was the situation at the end of the war.

Bullard moved against Ballou shortly after the Armistice, on
November 14, asking GHQ for the general's relief. Three days later
Pershing removed Ballou, transferring him to the Eighty-sixth
Division, a depot division that by that time was without troops.

General Ballou should have accepted this demotion because he
was in no position to do otherwise. Whatever his view of Bullard,
which was as low as it could be, he could not oppose a lieutenant
general. He showed his poor judgment again by sending a long effu-
sion to Pershing in which he sought, with near-complete lack of tact,
to set out his case. He began with a statement that was impossible,
considering his contention was with a lieutenant general: he said
that he trusted that an experienced military man without prejudice
against him personally would read his statement, and he hoped
the result would be a recommendation for an investigation of any

alleged inefficiency or misconduct on his part. He set out his reasons for not wishing the 367th Regiment to be sent across the Moselle to be placed next to the Seventh Division, pointing out that he desired the regiment in this event to be under command of the general of the Seventh Division. This was a good point, worth mentioning, but the Second Army had refused it and Ballou would have done better not to bring it up. He criticized General Barnum for not understanding that he, Barnum, after sending his two regiments against Bois Fréhaut and the smaller forests of Voivrotte and Cheminot, made no preparation to attack the towns above that defended the German position on the large hill in between. He criticized General Sherburne for incapacity—when Major Ross found the 167th Artillery Brigade gave excellent support during the attack on Fréhaut. He said almost nothing of the success of Ross's Second Battalion, 365th Regiment, in taking Fréhaut. He dwelled in excruciating detail on his presence behind Voivrotte. Sawkins commanded a force of three companies. He mentioned Cheminot, which involved two platoons. Ballou had no access to his former division's records and said he was writing from memory. His request went over the head of Bullard, direct to GHQ, and does not seem to have crossed Pershing's desk.

Bullard in the meantime was asking Pershing to send the Ninety-second home. He so wrote to Pershing, that he would like to be rid of Ballou or the division, preferably both, and accomplished the former first, the division a few weeks later when it commenced to move out of the sector. Because of the shortage in shipping, the Ninety-second did not begin to embark at Brest until January 30, 1919, and over the next weeks the entire division went back, the men quickly released and sent home. It was first among AEF divisions, the others departing two or three months and more later.

Enough complaints about the Ninety-second's record, pro and con, reached the War Department that Secretary Baker decided on a special inquiry, which opened in August 1919, under Colonel Rivers. It was an investigation into the 368th, its actions and inactions the center of concern for everyone. Too, the court-martial cases were still in limbo, the five convicted officers under arrest, death sentences impossible to carry out. On October 2, 1919, President Wilson suffered a paralytic stroke, from which he only partly recovered before he left the presidency in 1921. Rivers and a colleague, also a colonel, sought out every officer of the 368th the investigative team could find, traveled to their locations, interviewed them at length, and took the results, shorthand testimony, under the closest scrutiny, attempting to find out where blame lay.

The preface of the present book relates what inadvertently happened to this near-priceless body of testimony taken by the Rivers investigation, its citation in the War College's analysis of the division's work published in fifty booklets in 1923, circulation restricted for forty years. The testimony did assist Rivers in deciding that the army should drop all thirty of the cases. Secretary Baker wanted this recommendation, but there is no evidence that Rivers decided to recommend dropping all charges because Baker desired it; Rivers made up his own mind. Rivers's care in his inquiry revealed marked flaws in the court-martial proceedings against the three lieutenants and Captain Smith. There do not seem to have been stenographic notes of their trials, and one wonders about the testimony, although it was said to have been from at least one white officer in each trial and two black officers. Major Norris testified at the trials of his five court-martialed officers. Colonel Brown testified as an expert witness. Rivers found that testimony about two runners, Bugler Rufus Buford and Corp. Thomas Braxton, was introduced into the trial only of Second Lieutenant Johnston, not in the other cases, resulting in Johnston's sentence to life at hard labor.

The testimony of Buford was in regard to a message Major Norris might have sent to I Company just before the officers and men retreated on October 28, around noon. Corporal Braxton offered similar testimony about the retreat at six o'clock. According to the runners, they carried messages telling Captain Green to retreat. The only man who could have said for certain was the captain, and he was badly wounded that night and died shortly after. Use of the Buford and Braxton testimony in one trial, not the others, necessarily affected the verdicts of the others. In his report to Baker, Rivers recommended that "no further action be taken in the other matters covered in this report," that is, the cases of the men before reviewing boards.

Rivers arranged for Baker to send an advance copy of the secretary's proposed statement on the Ninety-second, the reason for the Rivers investigation, to Norris, to discover his reaction in advance of Baker's press release. The colonel was no fool at diplomacy:

Major Norris, who commanded the 3rd Battalion, is an able, self-contained man about forty years of age, of the law firm of Bouvier and Beale of New York. He started his service with no prejudice against the colored man, but as a result of his experience he became firmly convinced that as a rule competent officers can not be obtained from the colored race, and so expresses himself emphatically. I don't think the final disposition of the cases of the officers who were tried is of any moment to him, but any general statement might cause comment from him.[16]

Baker wrote a careful letter. Norris replied that the circumstances requiring a statement from Baker were deplorable but thought mention of the battalion's men recommended for the Distinguished Service Cross and for promotion would help. On November 8, 1919, a press release from the War Department gave out a statement by Baker in which he announced the decision to cease all action against officers accused of misconduct in the Argonne, members of the 368th Infantry, Ninety-second Division, and tossed the bouquets advised by the former Major Norris.

General Bullard in his first year of retirement in 1925 published an attractive book titled *Personalities and Reminiscences of the War,* in which he skewered the record of the Ninety-second and, generally, the usefulness of blacks, men and officers, in the military. He may have had some feeling for the fact that the African American division on November 10–11 made the only advance of any unit in the Second Army. The book inspired veterans of the Ninety-second to state their grievances to Congressman Martin B. Madden of Illinois. Madden was a leading member of the House of Representatives and chairman of the Finance Committee. He was apprised by unnamed veterans that the 368th went into the Argonne with no food and without water and that the white officers spent their time in dugouts, sleeping there while ordering the men forward, so he told the House.[17] Colonel Brown, then in the War Department, sent the testimony in the *Congressional Record* to Norris, who replied at once in a letter to Madden. For Norris, these untruths were easy to scotch, which he did with suitable courtesy, to the distinguished member of the House. Madden extended his remarks by putting Norris's letter in the *Record,* and that was that.[18]

## NOTES

### ONE  Training

1. At the beginning of American participation in the war, former president Roosevelt sought to organize a division, as he did in creation of the Rough Riders in 1898. The administration refused to allow it, as it would have drained off the better officers of the Regular Army. Wood turned against the Wilson administration months later when the general was about to take a division to France and was recalled from the docks: he did not understand that the individual who did not want him in France was General Pershing.

2. Arthur E. Barbeau and Florette Henri, *The Unknown Soldiers: Black American Troops in World War I*, 59.

3. After the war Colonel Ballou wrote privately about what he described as the "first fault" in organizing the Ninety-second Division, which was not accepting enough candidates at Des Moines, half as many officers as a division required, and in dropping the requirement of a college education for officers. "For the parts of a machine requiring the finest steel, pot-metal was required" (memorandum to Col. Allen J. Greer, March 14, 1920, *The Colored Soldier in the United States Army*, 86–91).

4. The following accounts of the camps are from *Ninety-second Division, 1917–1918*, 1–17.

5. Allan R. Millett, "Over Where? The AEF and the American Strategy for Victory, 1917–1918."

6. *Ninety-second Division*, 19.

7. See chapter 3, 49–69.

8. Quoted in Donald Smythe, *Pershing: General of the Armies*, 142.

9. *Ninety-second Division*, 20.

10. Ibid., 20–21.

11. Memorandum of August 29, 1918, box 44, 92nd Division historical, entry 1241, RG 120. Citations followed by record group numbers are from the National Archives, College Park, Maryland.

12. J. Edward Cassidy, "History of the 317th Engineers (Sappers)," 39ff, box 14, 92nd Division historical, entry 1240, RG 120.

13. Lieutenant Colonel Cassidy was attempting to show that black company officers, wherever placed, were a mistake. "The morale of the 92nd Division infantry was so low they would not perform the ordinary duties of trench 'housekeeping.' The personnel of the infantry regiments were practically the same as the engineers—so the only conclusion is that the difference was due to the officer personnel" ("History of the 317th Engineers [Sappers]," 46).

14. Maj. Max Elser interview by Col. T. R. Rivers, July 24–25, 1919, Washington, D.C., 6. "Report of Special Investigation (including testimony) conducted in the office of the Inspector General of the Army by Colonel T. R. Rivers, dated Sept. 30, 1919. Subject: Report of Investigation concerning the 368th Infantry," box 113, entry 390, RG 159. This was the investigation mentioned in the preface, vii–viii.

**TWO**  Argonne

1. Fred R. Brown, interview by Colonel Rivers, August 13, 1919, Washington, D.C., 22.

2. "It was a terrible job getting through that Boche wire. I have never seen anything to equal it. There were two or three kilometers of solid jungle mass of French and German wire in No Man's Land and throughout the German trench system which they had been working on for four years, and the whole country, except in the boyaus and trenches, was covered with this mass of barb wire and covered with second growth brush. The new growth had grown up through this barb wire and was absolutely impenetrable" (ibid., 6).

3. Elser interview, 25.

4. For the three battalions of the 368th Regiment, with reports of company officers, September 26–30, 1918, see box 10, 92nd Division historical, entry 1241, RG 120.

5. Rivers's final report of September 30, 1919, 46–47 (see chap. 1, n. 14).

6. For the runners, Elser interview, 41–42. For rear headquarters, 19: "The messages from F and G companies went to my original post of command. My liaison officers, through a miscarriage of messages or failing to get word in some way, got out of touch with me, and just how it happened I don't know, but these messages were not sent forward to me."

7. Ibid., 25.

8. He reported four men wounded and one gassed, not many casualties for heavy machine-gun fire. The reported victim of gas almost certainly was in error, unless gas had drifted over from the French subsector.

9. It seems clear that however judicious Colonel Rivers was, he gave the 368th's officers the benefit of the doubt. Rivers believed that on the twenty-sixth, the first day, the Second Battalion occupied too much front line at two kilometers. In some sense front lines are the fool's gold of the amateur strategist. After all, the four infantry regiments of the Ninety-second occupied a line of twenty-five kilometers at Saint-Dié.

10. *Ninety-second Division*, 28.

11. Brown interview, 8; Elser interview, 21.

12. Brown interview, 10.

13. Benjamin F. Norris, interview by Colonel Rivers, August 7, 1919, New York, 10.

14. Ibid., 10–11.

15. Smith interview, 2–5, 8–10, 12, 16–17.

16. Rivers asked, "Where was your battalion on the afternoon of the 28th? What happened to it finally?" Elser answered, "During this afternoon the companies were held together in front of the Finland trench and by preventing them from drifting past and by working with those who did get out of position, I attempted to maintain those companies in front of it with the idea of making the advance that was directed. I found it absolutely impossible. There was simply an overflow of men" (Elser interview, 26–27).

17. Brown interview, 14–15.

18. Capt. James T. Burns, interview by Colonel Rivers, August 9, 1919, Camp Upton, New York, 14.

19. Norris interview, 6.

20. Apart from Merrill's experience, and perhaps because of it, there was another factor in what proved the success of the First Battalion, offered by one of the major's company commanders, Atwood: "There had been quite a bit of friction in switching of officers in the other two battalions. There had been no switching to amount to anything in our battalion. The only change, one officer, was added to me while I was over there. It had a great deal to do with the morale of the men. They were thoroughly acquainted with the officers, had confidence in them" (Capt. H. G. Atwood, interview by Colonel Rivers, July 22, 1919, Washington, D.C., 8).

21. John N. Merrill, interview by Col. W. C. Babcock, August 5, 1919, Washington, D.C., 5–6. Colonel Babcock, Inspector General Department, was Rivers's assistant and did occasional interviews.

22. Ibid., 11.

23. Ibid., 23.

24. Ibid., 8.

25. *Ninety-second Division*, 31.

26. Merrill interview, 8.

27. Ibid., 9.

28. Atwood interview, 8.

29. *Ninety-second Division*, 32.

30. Colonel Brown to Adjutant General of the Army, November 15, 1918, appendix A, box 10, 92nd Division historical, entry 1241, RG 120; *Emmett J. Scott's Official History of the American Negro in the Great War*, 141; *92d Division: Summary of Operations in the World War*, 25.

31. Rexmond C. Cochrane, *The 92nd Division in the Marbache Sector*, 24. Edward M. Coffman has described the Cochrane gas studies as a reliance for German force and casualty levels against the U.S. Army in 1918.

**THREE**  Engineers and Artillery

1. For the last week of the war the entire regiment turned to heavy-gauge railroads.

2. Brig. Gen. John H. Sherburne to Col. H. A. Smith, "Use of Negroes in the U.S. Military Service," Army War College curricular archives, records section, file 127, 127<->12, U.S. Army Military History Institute, Army War College, Carlisle Barracks, Pennsylvania.

3. *Ninety-second Division*.

4. "History of the 317th Engineers (Sappers)" (see chap. 1, n. 12).

5. Robert H. Ferrell, *Collapse at Meuse-Argonne: The Failure of the Missouri-Kansas Division*.

6. "History of the 317th Engineers (Sappers)," 15–16, 20–22.

7. Ibid., 14e–14g.

8. Ibid., 14g.

9. Ibid., 12.

10. Ibid., 11–13.

11. Ibid., 32.

12. Ibid., 107.

13. Ibid.

14. Rexmond C. Cochrane, *Use of Gas in the Meuse-Argonne Campaign, September–November 1918*.

15. Charles H. Williams, *Sidelights on Negro Soldiers*, 48–49.

16. *Ninety-second Division*, 7.

17. Ibid., 18a.

18. Ibid., 9.

19. Sherburne went to the brigade on July 20. The 167th's first brigadier was John E. McMahon, present from October 1917 to April 1918. McMahon was promoted to major general and assigned to the Fifth Division, where his gross incompetence forced his removal by his corps commander, Maj.

Gen. John L. Hines, with the entire concurrence of General Pershing. He was followed in the 167th by Col. W. E. Cole. Both McMahon and Cole were Regular Army.

20. Sherburne to Smith, "Use of Negroes," 1.

21. Williams, *Sidelights on Negro Soldiers*.

22. Ibid., 170–71.

23. Ibid., 162.

24. "Brief History in the Case of Major General C. C. Ballou, N.A.," box 8, Pershing Papers, entry 22, RG 200.

25. Sherburne to Smith, "Use of Negroes," 2–3.

26. Ibid., 3, 4.


## FOUR  Marbache

1. Ballou to Col. Allen J. Greer, March 14, 1920, *Colored Soldier,* 86–91.

2. The best sources for the geography, apart from the 1:20,000 map in *92d Division: Summary of Operations in the World War,* are *Ninety-second Division* and Warner A. Ross, *My Colored Battalion.*

3. "History of the 317th Engineers (Sappers)," 124–25 (see chap. 1, n. 12).

4. A town of Norroy lay to the west of the Moselle, not to be confused with the village on the east side.

5. Ross, *My Colored Battalion,* 35–36, 47.

6. Ballou to Pershing, November 20, 1918, "Brief History" (see chap. 3, n. 24).

7. Cochrane, *92nd Division in the Marbache Sector.*

8. Cochrane believed that the Ninety-second's gas officers and corps and division gas officers never compared the Ninety-second to the work of gas officers in the Seventh Division, where gas casualties were much higher; this would have shown the Ninety-second's gas personnel that the division had done well and that the African Americans again failed to see their own achievements (ibid., 46).

9. Ibid.

10. Ibid., 72.

11. Ibid., 77.

12. Ross, *My Colored Battalion,* 35–36, 47.

13. In the 1920s a contention developed over whether after the battle of Saint-Mihiel it was possible for the First Army to have taken Metz, this presumably instead of taking most of its divisions to the Meuse-Argonne.

14. Cochrane, the gas expert, described the Second Army as a large-scale rehabilitation center (*92nd Division in the Marbache Sector,* 81).

15. For the Ninety-second Division the changes instituted by Heintzelman may well have been sending the 367th Regiment west of the Moselle. Heintzelman began organizing the Second Army on September 9, and Bullard became commander on October 12; the staff probably was full of ideas after a month of thought.

16. Pershing was a well-known pusher, and even after he handed over the First Army to Liggett, on October 16, when the new lieutenant general took over, the commander in chief showed up in his steam train and kibitzed. See Robert H. Ferrell, ed., *In the Company of Generals: The World War I Diary of Pierpont L. Stackpole*; and Allan R. Millett, *The General: Robert L. Bullard and Officership in the United States Army, 1881–1925*, 424.

17. Cochrane, *92nd Division in the Marbache Sector*, 61n.

18. *Bjornstad, Col. Alfred W., Hearings before the Committee on Military Affairs*, U.S. Senate, 68th Cong., 2nd sess.

19. Ibid., pt. 1, p. 261.

20. Williams, *Sidelights on Negro Soldiers*, 163.

21. Second Battalion, 365th Infantry, special report of operations, box 7, 92nd Division historical, entry 1241, RG 120.

22. Ross, *My Colored Battalion*, 30. The book agrees with Ross's after-action report. See also Walter R. Sanders's autobiography, "Woevre Valley," box 7, 92nd Division historical, entry 1241, RG 120.

23. Ross, *My Colored Battalion*, passim.

## FIVE Conclusion

1. Millett, *The General*.

2. Hay to Greer, April 13, 1919, *Colored Soldier*, 113–15. The entire miscellany in *Colored Soldier*—letters and documents—appears as appendices of No. 118 in Bernard C. Nalty and Morris J. MacGregor, *Blacks in the United States Armed Forces*, vol. 4. After Colonel Greer returned to the United States with the Ninety-second, he spent time at the War Department before going back to Germany to join the Army of Occupation, and while in the department sent letters to officers he thought might enlighten the department on the use of African Americans in the army.

3. Jackson to Greer, April 14, 1919, *Colored Soldier*, 127–28.

4. McMaster to Greer, April 28, 1919, misc. file 2552, Army War College.

5. Greer to assistant commandant, General Staff College, Washington, D.C., April 13, 1920, *Colored Soldier*, 110–12.

6. McMaster to Greer, April 28, 1919.

7. *Emmett J. Scott's Official History*. One of Scott's assistants in France,

Ralph Tyler, obtained a copy of this letter, and it had wide circulation in the African American press.

8. Williams, *Sidelights on Negro Soldiers*, 75.

9. Ibid., 76.

10. Ibid., 65.

11. Elser interview, 5.

12. Ballou to commanding general, IV Corps, "Brief History" (see chap. 3, n. 24).

13. Brown interview, 25.

14. Elser interview, 35.

15. Millett, *The General*, 428.

16. Memorandum by Rivers, October 23, 1919, deposited at the end of the interviews.

17. *Congressional Record,* January 4, 1926, 1440–44.

18. Ibid., February 4, 1926, 3337.

# BIBLIOGRAPHY

Alexander, Robert. *Memories of the World War, 1917–1918.* New York: Macmillan, 1931.

*American Armies and Battlefields in Europe.* Washington, D.C.: Government Printing Office, 1938.

Ayres, Leonard P., ed. *The War with Germany: A Statistical Summary.* 2nd ed. Washington, D.C.: Government Printing Office, 1919.

Barbeau, Arthur E., and Florette Henri. *The Unknown Soldiers: Black American Troops in World War I.* Philadelphia: Temple University Press, 1974.

Beaver, Daniel R. *Modernizing the American War Department: Change and Continuity in a Turbulent Era, 1885–1920.* Kent: Kent State University Press, 2006.

———. *Newton D. Baker and the American War Effort, 1917–1918.* Lincoln: University of Nebraska Press, 1966.

Bjornstad, Col. Alfred W., *Hearings before the Committee on Military Affairs.* U.S. Senate, 68th Cong., 2nd sess., 2 pts. Washington, D.C.: Government Printing Office, 1925.

Braim, Paul F. *The Test of Battle: The American Expeditionary Forces in the Meuse-Argonne Campaign.* Newark: University of Delaware Press, 1987.

Bruce, Robert B. *A Fraternity of Arms: America and France in the Great War.* Lawrence: University Press of Kansas, 2003.

Bullard, Robert Lee. *Personalities and Reminiscences of the War.* Garden City, N.Y.: Doubleday, Page, 1925.

Bullard, Robert Lee, and Earl Reeves. *American Soldiers Also Fought.* New York: Longmans, Green, 1936.

Chambers, John Whiteclay. *To Raise an Army: The Draft Comes to Modern America.* New York: Free Press, 1987.

Clifford, John Garry. *The Citizen Soldiers: The Plattsburg Training Camp Movement, 1913–1920.* Lexington: University Press of

Kentucky, 1972.

Cochrane, Rexmond C. *The 92nd Division in the Marbache Sector.* Washington, D.C.: U.S. Army Chemical Corps, 1959.

———. *The 78th Division at the Kriemhilde Stellung, October 1918.* Washington, D.C.: U.S. Army Chemical Corps, 1958.

———. *The Use of Gas in the Meuse-Argonne Campaign, September–November 1918.* Washington, D.C.: U.S. Army Chemical Corps, 1959.

Coffman, Edward M. *The Hilt of the Sword: The Career of Peyton C. March.* Madison: University of Wisconsin Press, 1966.

———. *The Old Army: A Portrait of the American Army in Peacetime, 1784–1898.* New York: Oxford University Press, 1986.

———. *The Regulars: The Army Officer, 1898–1941.* Cambridge: Harvard University Press, 2004.

———. *The War to End All Wars: The American Military Experience in World War I.* New York: Oxford University Press, 1968.

Colby, Elbridge. "The Taking of Montfaucon." *Infantry Journal* 47 (1940): 128–40.

*The Colored Soldier in the United States Army.* Washington, D.C.: War College, 1942.

*Congressional Medal of Honor, the Distinguished Service Cross, and the Distinguished Service Medal.* Washington, D.C.: Government Printing Office, 1920.

Cooke, James J. *The All-Americans at War: The Eighty-second Division in the Great War, 1917–1918.* Westport, Conn.: Praeger, 2002.

———. *Billy Mitchell.* Boulder: Lynne Rienner, 2002.

———. *Pershing and His Generals: Command and Staff in the AEF.* Westport, Conn.: Praeger, 1997.

———. *The Rainbow Division in the Great War.* Westport, Conn.: Praeger, 1994.

———. *The U.S. Air Service in the Great War, 1917–1919.* Westport, Conn.: Praeger, 1996.

Cramer, C. H. *Newton D. Baker: A Biography.* Cleveland: World, 1961.

Cunningham, Roger D. *The Black Citizen-Soldiers of Kansas, 1864–1901.* Columbia: University of Missouri Press, 2008.

DeWeerd, Harvey A. *President Wilson Fights His War: World War I and the American Intervention.* New York: Macmillan, 1968.

Dobak, William A., and Thomas D. Phillips. *The Black Regulars.* Norman: University of Oklahoma Press, 2001.

Doughty, Robert A. *Pyrrhic Victory: French Strategy and Operations in the Great War.* Cambridge: Harvard University Press, 2005.

Eisenhower, John S. D. *Yanks: The Epic Story of the American Army in World War I.* New York: Free Press, 2001.

Emmett J. *Scott's Official History of the Negro in the World War.* Chicago: Homewood, 1919.

Ferrell, Robert H. *America's Deadliest Battle: Meuse-Argonne, 1918.* Lawrence: University Press of Kansas, 2007.

——. *Collapse at Meuse-Argonne: The Failure of the Missouri-Kansas Division.* Columbia: University of Missouri Press, 2004.

——. *Five Days in October: The Lost Battalion of World War I.* Columbia: University of Missouri Press, 2005.

——. *Woodrow Wilson and World War I, 1917–1921.* New York: Harper and Row, 1985.

——, ed. *In the Company of Generals: The World War I Diary of Pierpont L. Stackpole.* Columbia: University of Missouri Press, 2009.

*Final Report of John J. Pershing: Commander-in-Chief, American Expeditionary Forces.* Washington, D.C.: Government Printing Office, 1920.

Fleming, Thomas J. *The Illusion of Victory: America in World War I.* New York: Basic Books, 2003.

Glasrud, Bruce A. *Brothers to the Buffalo Soldiers: Perspectives on the African American Militia and Volunteers, 1865–1917.* Columbia: University of Missouri Press, 2011.

Glasrud, Bruce A., and Michael N. Searles. *Buffalo Soldiers in the West.* College Station: Texas A & M University Press, 2007.

Grotelueschen, Mark E. *The AEF Way of War: The American Army and Combat in World War I.* New York: Cambridge University Press, 2007.

Gudmundsson, Bruce I. *Stormtroop Tactics: Innovation in the German Army, 1914–1918.* Westport, Conn.: Praeger, 1989.

Haber, L. F. *The Poisonous Cloud: Chemical Warfare in the First World War.* Oxford: Clarendon, 1986.

Harbord, James G. *The American Army in France, 1917–1919.* Boston: Little, Brown, 1936.

Hawley, Ellis W. *The Great War and the Search for a Modern Order: A History of the American People and Their Institutions, 1917–1933.* New York: St. Martin's, 1979.

Herwig, Holger H. *The First World War: Germany and Austria-*

*Hungary, 1914–1918.* London: Arnold, 1997.

Hunton, Addie, and Katherine Johnson. *Two Colored Women with the American Expeditionary Forces.* New York: Brooklyn Eagle, 1920.

Hurley, Alfred F. *Billy Mitchell: Crusader for Air Power.* Bloomington: Indiana University Press, 1975.

Keegan, John. *The First World War.* New York: Knopf, 1999.

Keene, Jennifer D. *Doughboys, the Great War, and the Remaking of America.* Baltimore: Johns Hopkins University Press, 2001.

Langer, William L. *Gas and Flame in World War I.* New York: Knopf, 1965.

Lentz-Smith, Adriane. *Freedom Struggles: African Americans and World War I.* Cambridge: Harvard University Press, 2009.

Liggett, Hunter. *A.E.F.: Ten Years Ago in France.* New York: Dodd, Mead, 1928.

——. *Commanding an American Army: Recollections of the World War.* Boston: Houghton Mifflin, 1925.

Little, Arthur W. *From Harlem to the Rhine: The Story of New York's Colored Volunteers.* New York: Covici, Friede, 1936.

Millett, Allan R. *The General: Robert L. Bullard and Officership in the United States Army, 1881–1925.* Westport, Conn.: Greenwood, 1975.

——. "Over Where? The AEF and the American Strategy for Victory, 1917–1918." In *Against All Enemies: Interpretations of American Military History from Colonial Times to the Present,* ed. Kenneth J. Hagan and William R. Roberts. Westport, Conn.: Greenwood, 1986.

Nalty, Bernard. *Strength for the Fight: A History of Black Americans in the Military.* New York: Free Press, 1986.

Nalty, Bernard, and Morris J. MacGregor, eds. *Blacks in the United States Armed Forces: Basic Documents.* 13 vols. Wilmington, Del.: Scholarly Resources.

Nenninger, Timothy K. "Unsystematic as a Mode of Command: Commanders and the Process of Command in the American Expeditionary Forces, 1917–1918." *Journal of Military History* 64 (2000): 739–68.

*Ninety-second Division, 1917–1918.* Washington, D.C.: War College, 1923.

*92d Division: Summary of Operations in the World War.* Washington,

D.C.: Government Printing Office, 1944.

*Order of Battle of the United States Land Forces in the World War: American Expeditionary Forces; General Headquarters, Armies, Army Corps, Services of Supply, Separate Forces.* Washington, D.C.: Government Printing Office, 1937.

Palmer, Frederick. *Our Gallant Madness.* Garden City, N.Y.: Doubleday, Doran, 1937.

———. *Our Greatest Battle (the Meuse-Argonne).* New York: Dodd, Mead, 1919.

Patton, Gerald W. *War and Race: The Black Officer in the American Military, 1915–1941.* Westport, Conn.: Greenwood, 1981.

Pearlman, Michael S. *Warmaking and American Democracy: The Struggle over Military Strategy, 1700 to the Present.* Lawrence: University Press of Kansas, 1999.

Pershing, John J. *My Experiences in the World War.* 2 vols. New York: Stokes, 1931.

Persico, Joseph E. *Eleventh Month, Eleventh Day, Eleventh Hour: Armistice Day, 1918, World War I, and Its Violent Climax.* New York: Random House, 2004.

Pitt, Barrie. *1918: The Last Act.* London: Cassell, 1962.

Pogue, Forrest C. *George C. Marshall: Education of a General, 1880–1939.* New York: Viking, 1963.

Rainey, James W. "Ambivalent Warfare: The Tactical Doctrine of the AEF in World War I." *Parameters* 13 (1983): 34–45.

———. "The Questionable Training of the AEF in World War I." *Parameters* 22 (1992–1993): 89–103.

*Report of the Secretary of War to the President, 1926.* Washington, D.C.: Government Printing Office, 1926.

Robinson, Charles M. III. *The Fall of the Black Army Officer: Racism and the Myth of Henry O. Flipper.* Norman: University of Oklahoma Press, 2008.

Ross, Warner A. *My Colored Battalion.* Chicago: Ross, 1920.

Shellum, Bruce G. *Black Officer in a Buffalo Soldier Regiment: The Military Career of Charles Young.* Lincoln: University of Nebraska Press, 2010.

Smith, Gene. *Still Quiet on the Western Front: Fifty Years Later.* New York: Morrow, 1965.

Smythe, Donald. *Guerrilla Warrior: The Early Life of John J. Pershing.* New York: Scribner, 1973.

——. *Pershing: General of the Armies*. Bloomington: Indiana University Press, 1988.

*Summary of Operations in the World War* [by divisions, separately published]. Washington, D.C.: Government Printing Office, 1943–1944.

*United States Army in the World War*. 17 vols. Washington, D.C.: Government Printing Office, 1948.

Vandiver, Frank E. *Black Jack: The Life and Times of John J. Pershing*. 2 vols. Fort Worth: Texas Christian University Press, 1977.

Van Every, Dale. *The A.E.F. in Battle*. New York: Appleton, 1928.

Venzon, Anne Cipriano, ed. *The United States in the First World War: An Encyclopedia*. New York: Garland, 1995.

Votaw, John F. *The American Expeditionary Forces in World War I*. Oxford: Osprey, 2005.

Weigley, Russell F. *The American Way of War: A History of United States Military Strategy and Policy*. New York: Macmillan, 1973.

——. *History of the United States Army*. New York: Macmillan, 1967.

Williams, Charles H. *Sidelights on Negro Soldiers*. Boston: Brimmer, 1923.

# INDEX

Alexander, Fritz, 101
Alexander, Levy, 101
Algeria, 39
Anderson, Clay, 51
Atwood, H. G., 18, 36, 39

Baer, J. A., 55–56
Baker, Newton D., 4, 32, 98, 103, 105–6
Ballou, Charles C., 4, 6, 13, 51–52, 54–55, 67–68, 72, 74, 77–82, 85, 89, 92, 99–104
Barnum, Malvern Hill, 68, 86, 104
Belgium, 10
Bettis, Benjamin, 101
Biddle, John, 52
Bjornstad, Alfred W., 81–84
Black, W. M., 52–53
Bliss, Tasker H., 52
Booth, E. E., 83
Boursault, Elizabeth, 13
Bouvier and Beale (law firm), 24
Braxton, Thomas, 105
Brown, Earl I., 51, 53–56, 59–63, 92
Brown, Fred R., 24–28, 31–33, 35–37, 39–40, 53, 100, 103, 105–6
Brown, Lytle, 53, 55
Browning machine guns, 7
Buford, Rufus, 105
Bullard, Robert L., 67, 70, 77–80, 82–85, 90, 99, 102–4, 106
Bump, A. L., 81, 83
Bundy, Omar, 79
Burns, James T., 32–33

Camps: Dix (N.J.), 8–9, 64–65; Dodge (Ia.), 7; Funston (Kans.), 6, 51; Grant (Ill.), 7; Meade (Md.), 8, 64; Sherman (Oh.), 7–8, 51, 55; Upton (N.Y.), 9, 54
Cassidy, J. Edward, 49, 51, 63, 90, 92
Chauchat machine gun, 7, 20
Cheers, H. W., 101, 103
Civil War, 91, 101
Cochrane, Rexmond C., 75–76, 82
Coleman, Frank, 16, 19
Commerce, Department of, 52
Congress. *See* House of Representatives; Senate
*Congressional Record*, 106
Crawford, H. W., 101, 103
Cross, Judge, 101, 103

Dawes, Charles G., 60
Degoutte, Jean, 83–84
Deitsch, Auswell E., 75
Democratic party, 4
Dent, Francis M., 101
Des Moines Officers Training School, 3–4, 7, 29, 31, 52, 55, 63–64
DuBois, W. E. B., 4
Duke, Mr., 53
Dunn, Col., 67, 70
Durand, Col., 25, 28–29, 34, 37–39

Eighty-eighth Division, 80
Eighty-seventh Division (French), 12

121